W9-AGF-580

PAT RICHARDS CRAFTS COLLECTION

GLORIOUS CHRISTMAS ORNAMENTS

PAT RICHARDS CRAFTS COLLECTION

GLORIOUS CHRISTMAS ORNAMENTS

MORE THAN 40 HANDMADE TREASURES FOR YOUR TREE

Photography by George Ross

FRIEDMAN/FAIRFAX
PUBLISHERS

A FRIEDMAN/FAIRFAX BOOK

Library of Congress Cataloging-in-Publication Data

Richards, Pat, 1957-
        Glorious Christmas ornaments.
                        p.   cm.—(The Pat Richards crafts collections)
        ISBN 1-56799-473-3
        1. Christmas decorations.   I. Title.   II. Series: Richards, Pat,
    1957-   Pat Richards crafts collections.
    TT900.C4R5325   1997
    745.594'12—dc21   96-37941
                                                          CIP

Project Editor: Francine Hornberger
Editor: Jackie Smyth
Art Director: Jeff Batzli
Designer: Gatta Design & Co
Photography Director: Christopher C. Bain
Photographer: George Ross
Photo Stylist: Karin Strom
Border Illustrations: Timothy Bush
Other Illustrations: Alan Andersen
Production Manager: Camille Lee

Color separations by Bright Arts Graphics (S) Pte Ltd.
Printed and bound in China by Leefung-Asco Printers Ltd.

Every effort has been made to present the information in this book in a clear, complete, and accurate manner. It is important that all instructions be clearly understood before beginning a project. Please follow instructions carefully. Due to the variability of materials and skills, end results may vary. The publisher and the author expressly disclaim any and all liability resulting from injuries, damages, or other losses incurred as a result of material presented herein. The author also suggests refraining from using glass, beads, or buttons on crafts intended for small children.

1 3 5 7 9 10 8 6 4 2

For bulk purchases and special sales, please contact:
Friedman/Fairfax Publishers
Attention: Sales Department
15 West 26th Street
New York, New York 10010
212/685-6610   FAX 212/685-1307

Visit our website:
http://www.metrobooks.com

Dedication

This book is dedicated to my family, especially Mark, Keith, and Lee, who join me in a race each Christmas to get our favorite ornaments in the best spots on the tree.

Special thanks to Amy Syrell who helped me by creating the Jumping Jack ornaments. Thank you also to the Brown Bag Cookie Art division of Hill Design Inc., who provided me with some of their wonderful cookie molds for use in this book, and to Duncan for supplying me with their superb paints.

Contents

Introduction

My mother still has, and displays each Christmas, the first ornament I ever made—a large papier mâché Santa head that was a class project in elementary school. It still has so much appeal that I included a version of it in my first book, 101 Christmas Crafts. Over the years my brothers and sisters and I created our share of ornaments, mostly of the Styrofoam ball and sequin variety.

By the time I was in high school, I was so enthralled by the holiday that I persuaded my parents to let me have my own small Christmas tree. I used precious babysitting dollars to buy a small stand and string of lights, which I still have, and set the tree up in my room. Decorations were fashioned from tissue paper and egg cartons, among other things. Thus, my passion for creating Christmas ornaments was well begun. I have been making ornaments ever since.

For a time I specialized in clothespin dolls: brides, Santas, angels, and dancers grace the branches of our tree. The clothespin dolls evolved into little pipe cleaner pixies which swing here and there along with painted clay hearts, tiny jack-in-the-boxes, and marbled picture frames. When I had the time, I put together a small collection of ornaments to sell at craft fairs and through mail order. Now I have assembled a whole new collection of ornaments with patterns and directions for you to re-create. With this book you can capture the magic of handmade ornaments for your own tree or for others—and they make excellent gifts.

Some of the projects in this book, like the cotton batting Santa, are patterned after very old ornaments. The Victorians made a variety of figures from this material. Others like the space ships, are brand new ideas that have sprung from my children's interests. Many of these ornaments, like the clay vegetables and pull toys, are easy to make. Others, like the carousel and the teapot, are more challenging but not truly difficult. Be sure to carefully read through chapter one for tips on working with different techniques and materials. Have fun creating these ornaments, and most importantly have a very merry Christmas!

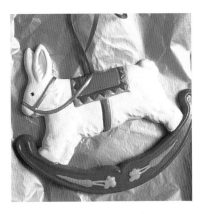

Before You Begin

Before You Begin

This chapter has been designed to provide you with tips on working with different techniques and materials. Be sure to read through it carefully to give yourself a solid background before embarking on any of these projects in the book.

>─◄►─◦─◄►─◄

PATTERNS

One of the best things about making Christmas tree ornaments is that the projects are rather small, and so the patterns are also small. Because of this, we were able to provide all necessary patterns full size. There is no need to run to the copy shop or to draft grids for enlargement.

You will find it helpful to keep tracing paper and a variety of template materials (i.e., lightweight cardboard, plastic) on hand for transferring the patterns from the page to the project.

MOLDS

Cookies and candy present great options for the beginning crafter who would like to make some special Christmas ornaments for him- or herself or to give as gifts. The mold provides the design, but it is up to the crafter where to go from there. Several ornaments in this book have been made with cookie molds provided to me by the Brown Bag Cookie Art division of Hill Design Incorporated (See Sources on page 116). They produce a large variety of molds and stamps and I have long been enamored of their wonderful designs.

NOTE

Many of the projects in this book call for the use of Styrofoam. In some cases, air-drying clay or papier mâché may be substituted.

GLUE

The choice of glue can be a source of confusion for many crafters, beginners and experienced alike. I keep a variety among my craft supplies. The glue I tend to use most often is a tacky white craft glue in a squeeze bottle; most brands are interchangeable. This type of glue works well on most all of my projects.

Sometimes, when I want a quicker grab, or when I am working with uneven surfaces such as Styrofoam, I will resort to an extra-thick and tacky glue in a tub, but I find it more wasteful as I rarely finish the container before the glue has dried up too much to use. I also keep a jewelry-type glue for attaching things like rhinestones. It is advisable to test the glue beforehand on the materials you propose to use it on as some of these glues will eat through the metallic backs of the stones, destroying the effect. Lastly, hot glue guns, and the newer low temperature glue guns, have become very popular in crafting, but for the projects in this book, they have few applications, because they may dispense too much glue too quickly.

Within the project instructions there are several instances where you are required to spread a thin layer of glue on a piece of paper or similar surface. This is best accomplished with the aid of a stiff card or, as I've been using, an expired credit card or plastic ID card. This allows you to effectively spread the glue in a very thin layer, which minimizes the bubbling and warping that occurs when the glue has been applied too generously.

PAINTS AND SEALERS

Paints can also cause confusion. I urge you to purchase a quality name brand. You will find that they go on smoother and hold up better in the long run. I have used Duncan paints for years, finding them to be an excellent product that goes on nicely and lasts well in the bottle. I am still using bottles I purchased four years ago. Duncan is currently producing a line of paints with Aleene's called Aleene's Premium Coat, which is available in a well-coordinated line of colors. (See Sources on page 116).

When crafting I tend to get very impatient to get on with the next step and I am sure there are many others like me out there. I cannot stress enough the importance of letting your project dry completely before proceeding to the next step. In my first attempts with the burnt brown paper technique, for example, I failed to let the glue dry thoroughly before painting and applying sealer. The surface remained sticky for so long I eventually had to throw the project out and start over.

Make sure to test various sealers, paints, and finishes for interactions. I had originally envisioned the clip-on mushrooms with a sparkle finish, but when I tried a spray glitter over a perfectly dry paint job the paint and/or clay softened and became very sticky and I had to forget about that idea.

Occasionally a product needs to be dried only to a certain tackiness. The gold size used on the gold-leafed bunny ornament and various crackle mediums are two examples. Pay close attention to the manufacturer's directions in each case in order to achieve the best results. It may also be advisable to test out an unfamiliar product or technique on a throwaway project before committing yourself to using it on your special ornaments.

CUTTING AND SANDING

Several of the ornaments in this book are made from Styrofoam which requires cutting. I found a small serrated saw designed for carving pumpkins to be an excellent tool for this purpose. A serrated kitchen knife also works well. When you need to smooth out the cut edges of a piece of Styrofoam, use the edge of a Styrofoam scrap. It works much like sandpaper on itself.

For sanding small projects I found an emery board a helpful alternative to sandpaper: it's stiffer and there's usually one handy somewhere in the house.

Several of the projects specify "scrap art" in the list of required materials. If you are a saver of Christmas cards and scraps of pretty papers you may need look no further. If not, investigate craft stores and bookstores for books of scrap art specially prepared for decoupage and crafts such as theses. I have several published by Dover Publications that come in handy when I'm creating. (See Sources on page 116).

Last but not least, many of the ornaments in this collection make use of eye pins for hangers. These can be found among the jewelry findings at any craft store. Hardware stores usually have a selection of screw eyes which could also be used, but the eye pins are often more delicate in appearance and therefore less obvious.

I hope these tips and hints are helpful in your crafting, and that you have as much fun re-creating these ornaments as I had in designing them.

C h a p t e r   T w o

All That Glitters

Gold and Silver Foil Balls

MATERIALS

- Clear plastic globes
- Metallic gold and silver acrylic paint
- Foiling glue (several brands are available, including 3-D Foiling Glue from Aleene's and Plexi 400 Stretch Adhesive from Jones Tones)
- Gold and silver foil
- Ribbon for hanging

Swirling lines of three-dimensional foiling glue lend interest to these simple plastic globes.

1. To make either ornament, coat ball with several coats of metallic paint (allowing to dry between coats) until color is smooth and even.

2. Following manufacturer's directions, apply glue to ball in desired pattern (see note) and set aside to achieve proper tack.

3. Lay foil, dull side down, over glue and rub until foil adheres to surfaces. Reposition foil and continue to rub gently until all surfaces of glue are covered with foil.

4. Thread ribbon through hanging loop of globe.

NOTE

The gold ball was decorated with large exaggerated S's scrolling from top to bottom of the globe and with a few extra swirls for embellishment.

The silver ball was decorated with a spiderweb design, working the vertical lines first, then the horizontal scallops between the verticals. Work one half of the ball at a time, applying the glue, then the foil, then decorate the opposite side of the ball. When all silver portions are complete, form spider with foiling glue. When set, cover with gold foil.

Gold Leaf Rocking Rabbit

MATERIALS

- Terra-cotta cookie mold (this one is Rocking Rabbit from Brown Bag Cookie Art; see Sources on page 116)
- Cotton linter (short fiber cotton pulp paper for paper making/casting)
- Blender
- Sieve
- Clean sponge
- Dish towels
- Shellac (see note)
- Quick-dry gold size
- Mineral spirits for cleaning brushes
- Composition gold leaf (see note)
- Ribbon or cord for hanging
- Paint brushes (one should be able to handle the rigors of shellac, size, and thinners. Another should be soft and fluffy for applying gold leaf)

Composition gold leaf is the secret behind the brilliant gold sheen of this rocking-horse rabbit.

>─┤◆〉─◇─〈◆├─≺

1. Fill blender container about half full with water. Tear one sheet of linter into small pieces and add to the water. Let soak about 20 minutes. Blend mixture with short bursts until no visible pieces remain. It should look like cloudy white pulp suspended in water. If your blender is straining at all, add more water. Pour mixture into sieve and allow to drain until water drips slowly.

2. Scoop pulp up loosely and pat into mold. Make sure you have all areas of mold loosely covered with pulp before compressing it more firmly. Compress pulp into all details of mold, making sure you have an adequate, but not overly thick layer of fiber filling the entire mold and extending over the edges. When all fibers have been pressed into place and as much of the remaining water as possible has been poured off, place mold on folded towel and use sponge to further press and absorb. When you have exhausted that method, use a second folded towel to remove as much water as possible.

3. At this point, you can set the mold aside to dry overnight, or put it into the oven at 150° F (65° C) for 3 hours. Or, you can dry it in the microwave, placing it in the middle and setting the oven on full power for 1 minute. After 1 minute, rotate the mold one half turn and set timer for 30-second intervals, rotating mold until paper is dry. Use oven mitts to handle mold as you turn and finally remove it from the oven. Use a thin-bladed knife to carefully lift edges of paper casting and peel it out of mold.

4. When casting is thoroughly dry, paint the area to be gold leafed with two or more coats of shellac, according to manufacturer's directions. You need the surface to be leafed to be thoroughly sealed or gold size will be absorbed and leaf will not adhere properly.

5. When shellac is dry, apply one even coat of gold size. This will dry to proper tackiness in about an hour. Test by touching lightly; it should be a little tackier than cellophane tape.

6. Lay gold leaf over tacky areas and lightly smooth into place with a paintbrush. Use scraps of leaf to fill in tears and missed spots. If there are places where the size was too dry to grab, wait 24 hours and then reapply size and leaf again.

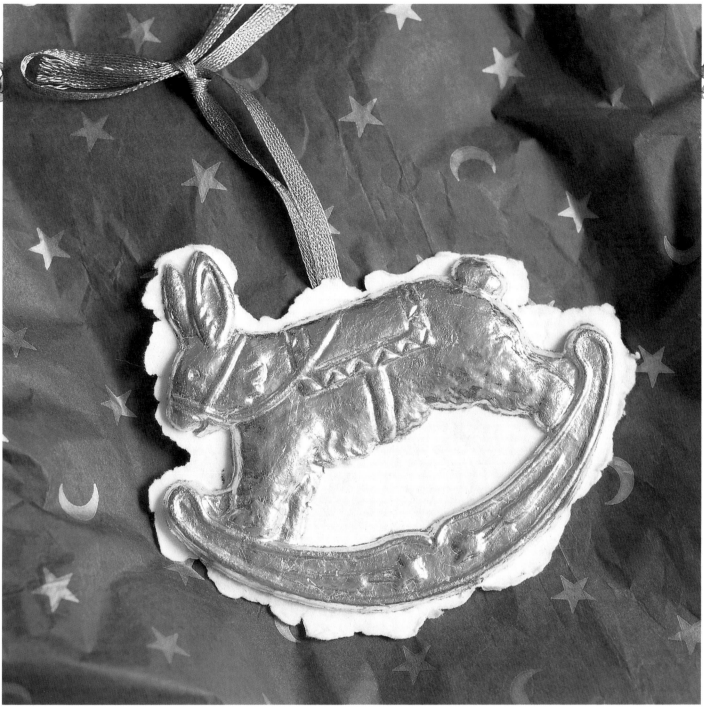

7. Polish with a tissue for smooth finish. Seal with another coat of size or with other clear finish to protect the delicate surface.

8. Glue a ribbon or cord to back for hanger and tie into a bow, if desired.

NOTE

Gold leaf is extremely delicate, expensive, and difficult to handle. Composition gold leaf is an imitation gold, somewhat easier to work with and much cheaper. Composition leaf can be handled with bare hands, if careful, or with a thin-bladed knife.

The shellac is used to seal the portion of the paper casting that is to receive the gold leaf. You may substitute several coats of acrylic paint if desired.

Icon Ornament

MATERIALS

- ✦ Postcard (see note)
- ✦ Tracing paper
- ✦ Cardboard
- ✦ Assorted trims and materials for embellishment
- ✦ Metallic gold and copper acrylic paint
- ✦ Small piece of sponge or bits of crumpled paper towel
- ✦ Clear finish or sealer, if desired
- ✦ Glue
- ✦ Gold cord

Fashioned to resemble intricately framed medieval art, these icon-type ornaments can be made from art postcards or recycled Christmas cards.

➤·◄◆➤·◆·O·◆·◄◆➤·◄

1. With tracing paper, trace the portion of the postcard that you would like to use on the ornament. At this point, decide if you want to alter the shape, perhaps into an arch, as I have done, or leave it as is. Use your tracing to work out the overall size of the frame you will now be creating. I made my frame approximately ½ inch (1.25cm) larger all around than the picture I was planning to use. Transfer this shape to the cardboard and cut out. Also cut out the portion of the postcard you are going to use. Mark the outer dimensions of the artwork onto the frame piece of cardboard.

2. Use your assorted trims now to create a three-dimensional frame for your artwork, outside of the traced line. For trim, use a length of braid or perhaps a row of pearls. I used a thin rope of air-drying clay, laid just outside the line, and flattened it at ⅛ inch (3mm) intervals with a toothpick to mimic the effect of a carved molding. When you are satisfied with the arrangement of trims, glue in place. Allow to dry.

3. When dry, paint the entire piece, front and back, with gold paint. Using the sponge or crumpled paper towels and working with both the gold and copper paints, add some dimension to the frame. Dip the sponge into gold and/or copper, work back and forth without cleaning the sponge, and apply the colors to the frame until you are happy with the effect. Allow the frame to dry.

4. When dry, apply a coat of sealer, if desired, then glue artwork to center of frame. Cut a piece of gold cord approximately 7 inches (18cm) long and glue ends to top back of ornament for hanging loop.

NOTE

These ornaments are intended to make use of materials you have available. I visited my art museum gift shop for postcards of medieval art against a gold background. You can usually find a picture of an angel or an illuminated manuscript that will suffice. The frames are rather catch as catch can. Use what you have on hand or visit a craft shop. The paint will bring the various elements together.

Stars and Spheres

MATERIALS

- ✦ 2 clear plastic globes in halves; one 4 inches (10cm), one 2¾ inches (7cm) in diameter
- ✦ Dark blue acrylic paint
- ✦ Metallic gold acrylic paint
- ✦ Toothpick and straight pin (optional)
- ✦ Clear drying glue
- ✦ Nylon thread

Gold stars applied freehand contribute to the celestial appeal of this ornament comprised of two spheres, one hanging by a nearly invisible thread within the second.

>─┤◆├─○─┤◆├─<

1. Paint inside of smaller globe with dark blue paint and set aside to dry. Note that the globe may take several coats of paint to achieve an even finish.

2. Paint gold stars in a variety of sizes on outside of larger globe. You can either paint stars freehand with a brush, or apply a dot of paint on the globe with the toothpick and use the straight pin to draw the points out from the center. When the blue paint is dry, paint some gold stars on the outside of the smaller globe as well.

3. Fit the two halves of the small globe together and seal the seam with a few tiny dots of glue. Knot a length of nylon thread through hanger and suspend smaller globe inside one half of large globe, adjusting until it hangs centered. Knot and glue thread to hanger of larger globe. It may be necessary to make a small nick into the flanges of the larger globe to accommodate the hanging thread and keep it centered. Fit the two halves of the larger globe together around the smaller globe, sealing the seam with tiny dots of glue.

25 All That Glitters

Satín Fabergé Ball

MATERIALS

- ☀ 4-inch (10cm) Styrofoam ball
- ☀ 12-inch (30.5cm) square of burgundy satin fabric
- ☀ 2 yards (2m) of gold cable cord
- ☀ Glue (extra thick and tacky is useful)
- ☀ Six ½-inch (1.5cm) flower-shaped studs
- ☀ 6 small rhinestones (optional)
- ☀ Twelve ⅜-inch (1cm) flower-shaped studs
- ☀ Thread
- ☀ Straight pin
- ☀ Tape measure
- ☀ Fine point marker
- ☀ Small screwdriver
- ☀ Tissue paper
- ☀ Gold eye pin for hanger

Inspired by the Fabergé eggs made around the turn of the century, this ornament is far more attainable. You can create it with Styrofoam and satin with a variety of jewelry accents.

>+·+>·O·<+·<

1. Insert straight pin into foam ball. Wrap thread around head of pin to anchor, then around ball to divide it in half. Mark along thread with fine-point marker. Remove thread and reposition to divide and mark each half into thirds (ball is now divided into six equal vertical sections).

2. With straight pin still located in original position, measure down and mark at 2 inches (5cm) and 4 inches (10cm) from pin on each dividing line. Connect the marks in lines that encircle the ball horizontally, dividing it into 18 segments.

Satin Fabergé Ball Pattern Pieces

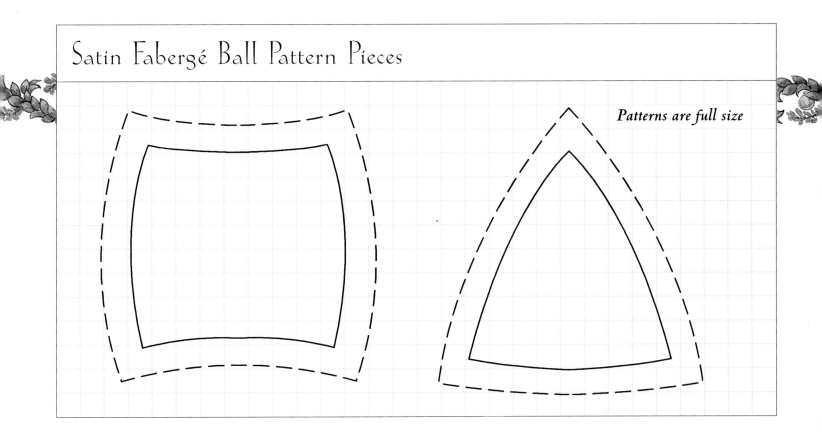

Patterns are full size

3. With a blunt, round-tipped object, such as a knitting needle or the end of a paintbrush handle, go over the lines, impressing them into the foam.

4. Trace above pattern pieces to tissue paper and use tissue pattern to cut 6 rectangular pieces and 12 triangular pieces from the burgundy satin.

5. Starting with the rectangular pieces, lay one piece over a corresponding section on the foam ball, having more or less equal allowances all around. With the screwdriver, poke the allowances into the ball along impressed lines. It helps to give yourself a little slack all around as you work. In other words, use the screwdriver to push the edges of the fabric toward the center of the section before pushing into the foam. Otherwise, when you go to poke in the opposite sides, the fabric will pull out of the sides already worked. You don't have to be exact since many rough edges and seams will be hidden when the cord is glued on. When the rectangular pieces are in place, continue in the same manner with the remaining pieces until the entire ball is covered.

6. Cut pieces of gold cord, one segment wide at a time, to fit in the horizontal seams. Apply glue to the seam and press the cord into the ditch, poking the ends into the ball. When all the horizontal segments have been worked, work four of the vertical dividing lines in segments that go halfway around, leaving one complete circumference to be worked last.

7. Position a large flower-shaped stud into the center of each rectangular section on ball and press into foam. If desired, glue a small rhinestone to the center of each stud. Position smaller flower studs in the center of each triangular section and press into ball. Trim eye pin to ½ inch (1.25cm) long. Insert and glue into top of ball.

Stained Glass Globe

MATERIALS

* Large, clear plastic globe

* Gold metallic relief outline paint for glass (imitation leading)

* Stained glass paint in three colors that can be applied to a vertical surface (I used red, purple, and green)

* Two large rubber bands

* Cord or ribbon for hanger

A clear plastic globe was transformed into a kaleidescope of color with the application of acrylic stained-glass paints. Here a simple geometric pattern has been used, but your imagination is the only limit to how your ball can be decorated.

>—I—◆>—O—<◆—I—<

1. Stretch rubber bands around center of globe, evenly spacing them about 1 inch (2.5cm) apart. Apply a line of gold dimensional paint along outside edge of each rubber band. When paint has set or dried thoroughly, remove rubber bands.

2. Referring to the leading diagram on the bottom of the next page as necessary, apply the relief paint in vertical lines from each of the horizontal lines up to the nearest point (top or bottom). It is easiest to first paint along the sides where you can follow the seam of the ball. Pick a point halfway between those two lines and draw a line from there to the center point in the same direction. Then draw a point halfway between those two. One half of the ball will now be divided into four equal segments. Those four segments will then be divided in half again, but these lines will not extend all the way to the center point; they end about ½ inch (1.25cm) short and are angled to meet the line next to it. These short lines at the top will form an eight-pointed star when the entire piece is completed. Work one-quarter of the ball at a time, and allow the area to dry before proceeding to the next quarter.

3. When all the dividing lines have been completed, paint the diamonds between the horizontal lines. Start at one vertical line and proceed to points halfway between the top and bottom vertical lines on either side of the starting point (refer to leading diagram on page 29 as necessary). The line should return to the vertical one directly below the starting point. These lines can be worked freehand, as stained glass is never perfectly precise.

4. When the dimensional painting is completed, begin to apply the color inside the lines. Alternate the red and purple in the vertical stripes, using emerald green in the diamonds. Work approximately one-eighth to one-fourth of the ball at a time, setting it down to dry before proceeding. Check the manufacturer's directions for curing time. My paint dried within approximately 8 hours, but took a week to cure, so I could continue to apply paint in sections. If I touched the previously applied paint for any length of time, however, it left fingerprints. When painting is complete, hang the ball somewhere undisturbed for a week.

5. Thread cord through loop for hanger and tie.

Stained Glass Globe Leading Diagram

Diagram is full size

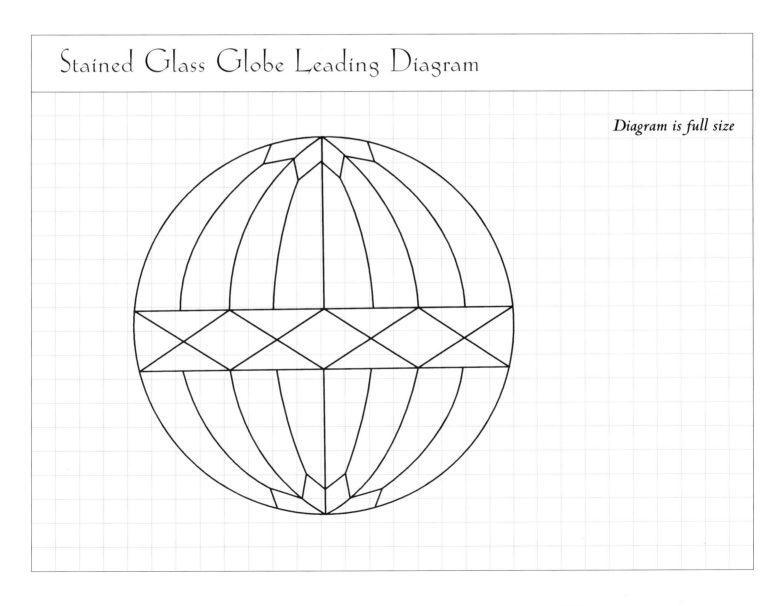

Burnt Brown Paper Star

MATERIALS

- Lightweight cardboard
- Brown kraft paper
- Tacky white glue
- 16-gauge craft wire
- Candle
- Metallic gold paint or wax paste
- Clear finish
- Eye pin
- Cord or ribbon for hanger

Who would have guessed that brown kraft paper and white glue could create such an effect? This gold star was made from burning a thick layer of glue applied to the brown paper. It's a great technique—a secret to keep to yourself or share with a friend.

1. Trace star pattern on the next page to lightweight cardboard and cut out.

2. Apply a thin layer of glue to one side of cardboard star and place glue side down on brown paper. Cut brown paper 1/8 inch (3mm) outside cardboard.

3. Apply glue to edges only on back of brown paper star, leaving a 2-inch (5cm) gap along one edge. Seal edges of star to another piece of brown paper, and cut out along outline of brown paper star.

Burnt Brown Paper Star Pattern

Diagram is full size

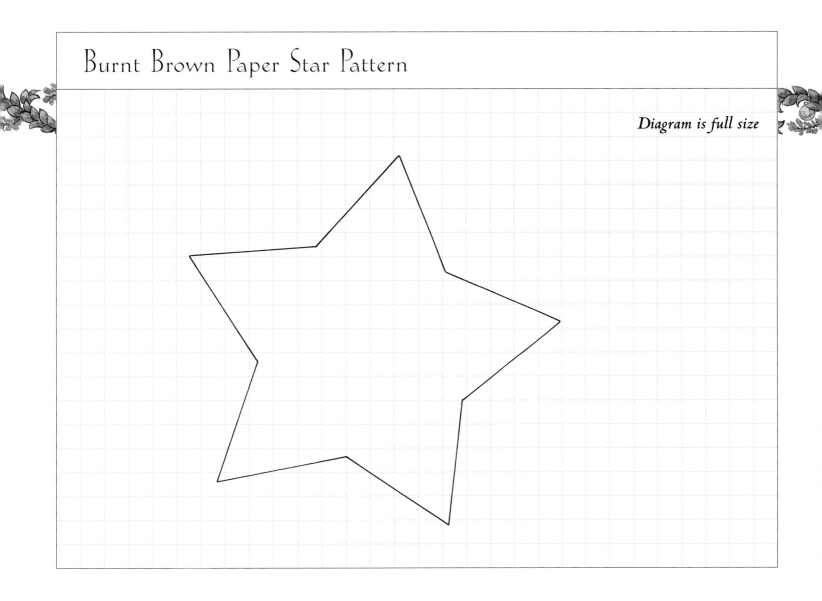

4. Cut an 18-inch (45.5cm) length of wire, fold in half, and twist together. Slip inside star.

5. Apply a thick, even coat of glue to one side of star. Light candle and place on a safe surface. Hold star by wire with glue side very close to flame and let the flame cause the glue to bubble and blacken. When surface is entirely blackened, extinguish the flame and let star cool. Carefully apply glue to opposite side of star and repeat the procedure. Set aside to cool.

6. With fingers or tissue, gently and carefully rub soot off surface.

7. Glue bottom of star together where wire was inserted.

8. Apply a thin line of glue to make decorative swirls on front of star. Set aside to dry completely. Glue should no longer be sticky.

9. With finger, apply gold wax to surfaces of star, taking care not to fill in all of the surface texture. Finish with two or more coats of clear finish. Trim eye pin to 1/2 inch (1.25 cm). Insert and glue to top point of star. String cord or ribbon through eye pin to create hanger.

NOTE
This project involves working with an open flame.
Be cautious when crafting with children.

Sun Globe

MATERIALS

- 3⅛-inch (8cm) clear plastic globe in halves
- Gold foil and foiling glue (see note)
- Dark blue acrylic paint
- Clear drying glue (optional)
- Cord or ribbon for hanger (optional)

The shimmering gold lines of this stylized sun stand in startling contrast to the dark blue background and transform an ordinary globe into something extraordinary.

>─┤◆>─O─<◆┤─<

1. Trace face pattern below and center it inside one half of globe. Apply foiling glue over the lines on the outside of globe. Set aside to partially dry and repeat the procedure with the opposite half of the globe.

2. When the glue has set somewhat, trace and position the sunbeam below inside one globe half at top of face. Apply glue over lines as before. Reposition sunbeam pattern and apply glue to either side and at bottom of face.

3. Between these sunbeams, work a freehand triangular sunbeam beginning at the outermost point, midway between two beams and pulling the line of glue to the point where the other sunbeams join the face. When sunbeams have been applied, set globe halves aside to dry according to manufacturer's directions.

Sun Globe Face and Sunbeam Patterns

Patterns are full size

Face

Sunbeam

4. When glue has set, lay foil, shiny side up, over design and rub over the glue lines to adhere the foil to the design. You can rub again to adhere foil to any spots missed.

5. Paint inside of globe halves with blue paint. Several coats may be necessary to achieve an even cover. When paint has dried, fit the two halves together, sealing the seam with a few dots of glue, if desired.

6. Tie ribbon or cord through hanging loop on globe and finish as desired.

NOTE

Several brands of gold foil and foiling glue are available, such as 3-D Foiling Glue from Aleene's and Plexi 400 Stretch Adhesive from Jones Tones.

Sun and Moon Disk

MATERIALS

* Sun and Moon cookie stamp (this one is from Brown Bag Cookie Art; see Sources on page 116)

* Salt dough (see recipe)

* Acrylic paints

* Satin finish sealer

* Gold cord for hanging

Simple salt dough and a cookie stamp team up to create this stunning medallion, made more dramatic with bold blue and metallic gold and silver paints.

1. Form a 2-inch (5cm) ball of salt dough (see recipe) and flatten slightly between hands. Flour lightly on both sides and place on baking sheet. Lightly dust cookie stamp with flour and center over dough, flattening it with even pressure until dough extends a scant 1/4 inch (6mm) around edges of stamp. Lift stamp straight up and off dough. If it sticks, roll dough up and try again with a little more flour, dusting until a good impression is achieved.

2. Trim edges of dough to approximately 1/4 inch (6mm) beyond design. Use a toothpick or pin to make a small hanging hole at top of design.

3. Preheat oven to 225°F (107°C). Bake ornament in center of oven for 30 minutes. Transfer directly to oven rack and bake for an additional one and a half hours until dry and hard. Cool on rack.

4. When ornament is completely cool, paint as desired with acrylic paints. Finish with two or more coats of satin sealer, allowing the first to dry before applying the second. Thread with cord for hanging.

SALT DOUGH RECIPE

2 cups (240g) flour, plus extra flour for dusting
1/2 cup (60g) salt
3/4 cup (100g) cold water

Mix flour and salt together, add the water, and stir until the flour is incorporated. Turn the dough onto a smooth surface and knead for about 5 minutes.

Wire-Wrapped Ornaments

MATERIALS

* Styrofoam ball or egg in desired size

* White tissue paper

* White glue

* Acrylic paint

* Crinkle wire (available from D. Blumchen; see Sources on page 116). You may substitute a fine metallic cord or thread, if desired

* Metallic trims cut from doilies, shelf trimming paper, and the like

* Eye pins and straight pins

RED AND GOLD EGG:
* 1/2 yd (46cm) of 1/2-inch-wide (1.5cm) gold wire-edged ribbon

PURPLE AND SILVER BALL:
* Thin silver cord

* 1 skein of 1/4-inch-wide (6mm) silver-wired tinsel garland (available from D. Blumchen). Metallic chenille stems may be substituted, if desired

The use of fine crinkled wire dates back to the earliest Christmas tree ornaments produced. Here it is the what makes these easy-to-make ornaments spectacular.

>‡◆>‑O‑<◆‑‡<

NOTE
The first five steps are for both ornaments. The directions to make each individual ornament follow step 5.

1. Tear tissue paper into squares approximately 1 inch (2.5cm).

2. Squeeze a small amount of glue into a dish and thin with water until a brushable consistency is achieved. Brush glue onto Styrofoam and cover with tissue paper, brushing glue mixture over edges of tissue to adhere to foam. Continue to cover with paper and glue, overlapping edges until entire shape is covered. You may want to do half at a time, letting piece dry in between so your fingers don't stick to the covered surfaces and lift the paper. Set aside to dry completely.

3. Lightly press in any bumps that appear and give covered foam two coats of desired color of acrylic paint, allowing the first coat to dry before applying the second.

4. When painted shape is dry, clip eye pin to about 3/4 inch (2cm) and insert at top of egg; use a straight pin if you are working on the ball ornament. Insert a straight pin directly opposite the top pin on bottom of foam shape. Leave pins protruding about 1/8 inch (3mm). Wrap one end of crinkle wire around the head of the top or bottom pin to secure. Then wrap wire, stretching it to desired effect as you go, to opposite pin, around pin, and back down the shape a short distance away from first wire to beginning pin, wrapping that pin and continuing up again. Keep wrapping shape with wire, anchoring it to top and bottom pins and working your way around shape. When you are satisfied with the appearance, wrap wire tightly around pin and clip. Apply a dot of glue to anchor wires at top and bottom and push pins into foam a bit to minimize any possible unsightliness of wrapped wiring.

5. Finish as follows.

RED AND GOLD EGG-SHAPED ORNAMENT
The red and gold egg is decorated with medallions cut from a doily and backed by a circle of pleated gold foil paper. Make a bow around a second eye pin and glue it in place to pin. Thread straight end of eye pin through eye pin on top of egg and twist to secure. Clip off excess length if necessary. Thread cord for hanging through upper loop on eye pin.

PURPLE AND SILVER BALL

The purple and silver ball is wrapped with a piece of silver shelf paper trim that was purchased by the yard from a baking supply store.

To make tassel: fold an index card in half, wrap thin silver cord around it 50 times. Cut a 6-inch (15cm) length of cord and tie tightly around top folds of wound cord. Cut through folds of cord opposite tie. Wrap tied end of cords several times with another piece of cord about 1/4 inch (6mm) below fold. Draw end of wrapping cord through the last wrap and glue to hold. Trim cord close to glue. Tie tassel securely to bottom pin and glue to reinforce knot. Trim ends close to pin.

Cut a 9-inch (23cm) length of wired tinsel garland and fold in half gently to form a

loop about 3 inches (7.5cm) long. Twist strands together to hold. Curl up the ends. Cut two 1-inch (2.5cm) lengths of 24-gauge craft wire and bend in half. Glue shaped garland to top of ball. Position one piece of folded wire over spot where one curl touches ball, and push into ball with fold of wire placed over garland to hold it more securely. (Basically you are putting a staple over the garland where it's glued to the ball.) Repeat with remaining wire reinforcement.

Cut a 4-inch (10cm) length of wired garland and gently fold in half. Twist fold around bottom pin, securing wires and tassel, and glue in place. Curl ends back toward ball and glue them in place. Cut two more 1-inch (2.5cm) pieces of wire, bending and pressing them into place over the bottom curls same as for top.

Chapter Three

Here Come the Animals

Follow the Leader

MATERIALS

- Yellow pom-poms: two ¼ inch (6mm), three ½ inch (1.5cm), and one 1 inch (2.5cm) in diameter
- Glue
- Covered floral wire
- Orange, black, and dark green acrylic paint
- Orange marker
- Small scrap of paper
- Large spring clothespin
- Spray sealer (optional)

This jaunty little family of pom-pom chicks perched on a spring-clip clothespin will bring a smile to the face of even the grumpiest Scrooge.

>—•‹›—O—‹›•—<

1. Glue ¼-inch (6mm) pom-poms on top of ½-inch (1.25cm) pom-poms, and remaining ½-inch (1.25cm) pom-pom to top of 1-inch (2.5cm) pom-pom.

2. With marker, color both sides of paper orange. Fold paper in half and cut two small and one larger triangular beak along fold. Glue beaks to smaller pom-poms of each assembly.

3. With a pin and black paint, give each chick two eyes above beak.

4. Paint wire orange. Cut two 2-inch (5cm) lengths and one 3-inch (7.5cm) length of wire. Fold each length in half, and after allowing approximately ½ inch (1.25cm) for each leg, fold remaining wire into small bird foot. Glue legs to bottom of each chick.

5. Paint clothespin green. When dry, finish with a spray sealer, if desired. Glue large chick to front of clothespin and two smaller chicks behind.

41 Here Come the Animals

Fishy Bag

MATERIALS

- Approximately 6-by-4-inch (15 by 35.5cm) piece of gray print fabric
- Scraps of red print and turquoise print fabrics
- Matching threads
- Small piece of thin batting or a scrap of flannel fabric
- 18 inches (45.5cm) of thin silver cord
- Two 1½-by-3½-inch (4 by 9cm) pieces of tear-away stabilizer

Scraps of colorful fabrics come together to make a delightful little satchel that can hide a tiny gift, or just brighten up your tree.

>─┤─◆─├─○─┤─◆─├─<

1. Adding ¼-inch (6mm) seam allowances to patterns provided on the next page, cut four bodies from gray print, four lower fins and two upper fins from red print, and two tails from turquoise print. Cut a tail from batting or flannel scrap. Transfer markings for eyes and fins to body front and back. Remaining two pieces are for lining.

2. With right sides together, sew around outer edges of each pair of fin pieces, using ¼-inch (6mm) seams and leaving dotted edges open. Clip curves and turn right side out.

Turn remaining ¼ inch (6mm) seam allowance of lower fins to inside and finger press. With matching thread, topstitch lines, approximately ⅛ inch (3mm) apart, in direction indicated on patterns on each fin.

3. With right sides of tail pieces together, and the batting or flannel on one side, sew around side and fluted edges. Trim batting or flannel close to seam. Clip curves and corners and turn tail right side out. With matching thread, work lines of topstitching as indicated on pattern on page 43.

4. Fold each piece of stabilizer in half and position one piece behind each marked eye. With sewing machine set on satin stitch, work center of eyes in red, outlining each with a border of turquoise. Tear away excess stabilizer. Pin lower fins in place on either side of body. With machine set on narrow zigzag, sew fins in place along top edges.

5. Pin upper fin in place to one body section, and tail in place to remaining body section. If desired, baste the tail and fin in place by hand. Pin the two body sections with right sides together. Making sure outer edges of tail and fins do not get caught in the seams, sew along side and tail edges using a ¼-inch (6mm) seam. Turn right side out. Sew body lining pieces together along the same edges. Trim seams and slip inside completed body, aligning seams and raw edges.

6. From remaining turquoise fabric, cut two bias strips, each 1 by 3½ inches (2.5 x 9cm), to finish raw edges of mouth. Working from the right side, fold under ¼ inch (6mm) at

end of one strip and place folded end even with side seam. With raw edges of fish, lining, and bias strip even and using a ¼-inch (6mm) seam, sew by hand along edge of mouth, almost to next side seam. Fold back edge of strip to meet seam and finish off. Work remaining edge with second strip in the same manner. Fold bias strips to the inside, turning under raw edge ¼ inch (6mm) and slipstitch in place.

7. With a large-eyed needle, thread silver cord through bias strip casing, pulling out hanging loops at each side seam. Stitch folded ends of bias strips together as invisibly as possible, leaving just enough room for cords. Knot and trim the ends of the cord to desired length.

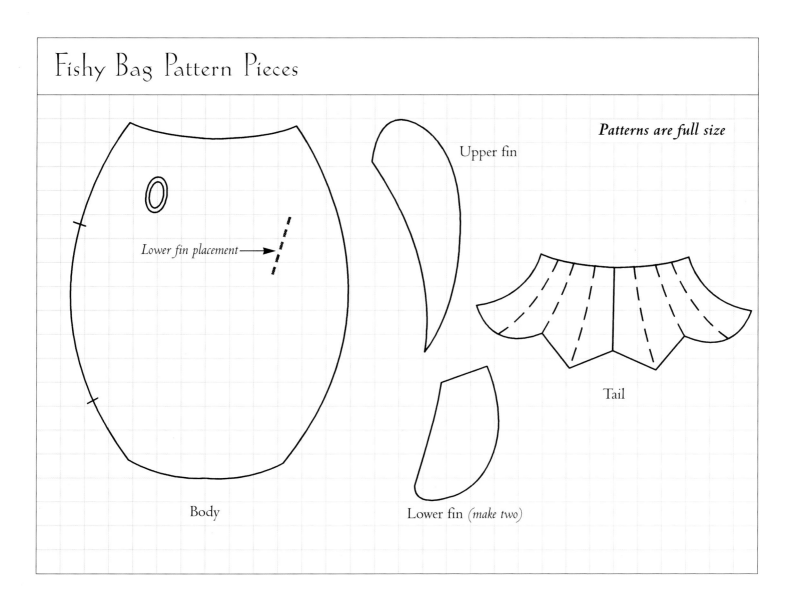

Fishy Bag Pattern Pieces

Patterns are full size

Upper fin

Lower fin placement ⟶

Tail

Body

Lower fin *(make two)*

Stuffed Twisting Snake

MATERIALS

* Scraps of assorted fabrics
* 18-gauge craft wire
* Fiberfil stuffing
* Scrap of red felt
* Small beads (optional)

A wire inside this bright and sinuous charmer allows him to hang curled from a branch to surprise the unwary viewer.

1. For each segment of snake, cut out one 1½-by-3-inch (4 by 7.5cm) piece of main color, one 1-by-3-inch (2.5 by 7.5cm) piece of contrasting color. Sew stripes together alternately along long edges. Along its length, fold strip in half, right sides together, and sew the side seam. Roll the seam to the center of the tube and sew around the end of the body that is in the main color, curving the stitching around the bottom for the tail. Turn the tube right side out.

2. Trace snake head pattern at left onto wrong side of main color fabric. Cut out two head pieces, adding ¼-inch (6mm) seam allowance around sides and top. With right sides together, sew around marked seam line, leaving neck edge open. Clip curves and turn right side out.

3 Turn under ½ inch (1.25cm) on one end of wire. Slip inside snake body all the way to the tail and fill space around wire with stuffing. Trim wire to 3 inches (7.5cm) beyond body and bend top 1½ inches (4cm) down on itself. Slip head over wire and stuff. Fold under ¼ inch (6mm) on snake body and slipstitch over neck edge of snake head. Cut a small forked tongue from felt and glue to head. Glue on beads for eyes, if desired.

NOTE
Snake can be made in various lengths depending on how many segments you opt to include; the snake shown here was made with seven segments.

Stuffed Twisting Snake Head Pattern

Pattern is full size

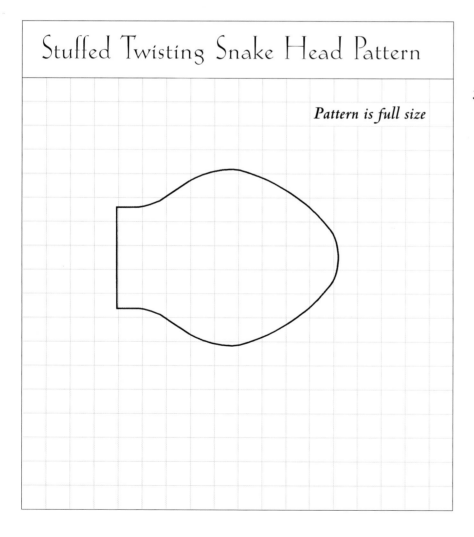

Flying Pig

MATERIALS

- Terra-cotta cookie mold (this one is Flying Pig from Brown Bag Cookie Art; see Sources on page 116)
- Salt dough (see recipe)
- Vegetable oil
- Flour
- Baking sheet
- Acrylic paints
- Crackle medium
- Sparkle varnish
- Ribbon for hanger

Christmas ornaments can run the gamut from the very traditional to the very unconventional, as in the case of this flying pig made from salt dough and a terra-cotta cookie mold.

>+↔>–O–<↔+<

1. Lightly oil cookie mold. Break off a piece of dough and, using fingers, press into all details of mold as evenly as possible. Pull dough back slightly from edges of mold. Holding mold vertically, rap edge of mold several times on cutting board. Turn mold over and carefully remove dough. Lay ornament flat on baking sheet.

2. Heat oven to 225° F (110°C). Place ornament in center of oven and bake 30 minutes. Transfer ornament directly to oven rack and continue baking an additional 1½ hours until ornament is totally dry and hard. Cool on rack.

3. Paint cooled ornament with white or ivory paint and set aside to dry. Following manufacturer's directions, apply crackle medium. When crackle medium is set, paint ornament as desired. To achieve an antique effect, paint pig with a light wash of brown paint wiping off excess. When dry, finish with a coat of sparkle varnish. Glue a loop of ribbon to back for hanger.

SALT DOUGH RECIPE

2 cups (240g) flour, plus extra flour for dusting
½ cup (60g) salt
¾ cup (100g) cold water

Mix flour and salt together, add the water, and stir until the flour is incorporated. Turn the dough onto a smooth surface and knead for about 5 minutes.

3. With a sharp needle, make a small hole at points indicated on body and leg pieces. Thread head pins from back of lower leg pieces through upper leg pieces and, using needle-nose pliers, twist a tight loop to hold in place, clipping off excess pin. Working pins in the same direction, thread through back of body, and then through each upper leg at point indicated on pattern. Join legs with cord as shown in assembly diagram also on page 49. Cut a 5-inch (13cm) length of cord for pull cord and tie to center point of cord, joining legs and allowing cord to hang down from body.

4. Cut seven ¼-by-½-inch (6mm by 1.25cm) pieces of basswood or cardboard. Glue one piece to inside of head on one body piece. Glue remaining pieces together in sets of two. Glue one set on inside of chest area, one inside rump area, and last set to back at hanging point. Glue a loop of cord around this block for hanger. Position body front over back, threading pins through matching holes and gluing to blocks set inside head, chest, and rump and twisting ends of eye pins to hold in place.

Jumping Jack Horse

MATERIALS

→ ¹/₃₂ inch (1mm) basswood or lightweight cardboard

→ Sharp craft knife (Exacto or a similar knife)

→ Sandpaper

→ White and gold acrylic paint

→ Floral scrap art or stickers

→ Glue

→ Satin finish sealer

→ Eight head pins (jewelry findings)

→ Needle-nose pliers

→ Cord

→ Small bead

→ Sharp needle

Modeled after the jumping jack toys that amused us as children, this ornament, cut from lightweight wood will charm young and old alike.

>—+—◆—◇—◆—+—<

1. Trace patterns (on page 49) and transfer each piece to basswood or cardboard and cut out with sharp craft knife. Cut two head/body pieces. Lightly sand edges, if necessary.

2. Paint both sides of each body piece white and allow to dry. Transfer saddle and bridle markings to opposite sides of body pieces. Paint bridle, saddle, and hooves with gold paint, as desired. Cut around selected scrap art and glue in place to body pieces along neck and back. Finish each piece with two or more coats of satin sealer.

Jumping Jack Horse Pattern and Assembly Diagram

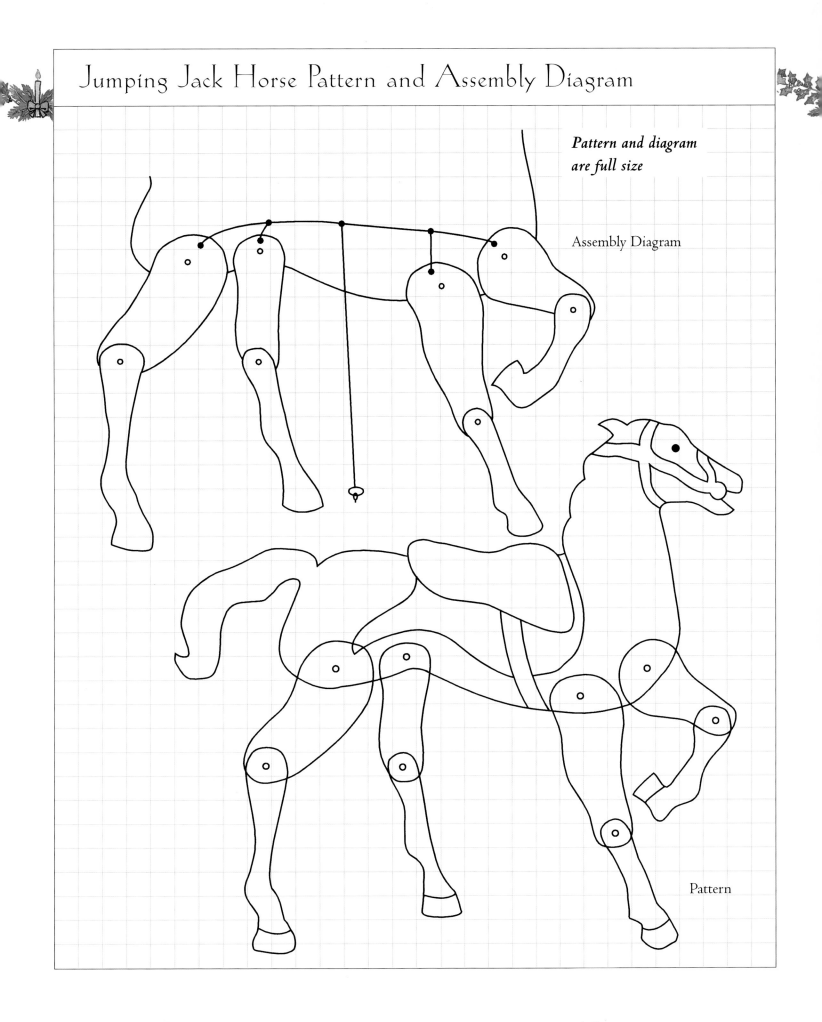

Pattern and diagram are full size

Assembly Diagram

Pattern

Jumping Jack Rooster

This cross-stitch jumping jack rooster ornament will be a delightful addition to your Christmas tree.

⤳ ┤ ◆ ─O─ ◆ ├ ↞

1. Following the chart on the next page, cross-stitch rooster onto perforated paper using three strands of embroidery floss in colors indicated. Outline all areas not bordered by black with one strand of black floss.

2. Lightly glue completed embroidery to white paper. Using sharp scissors, cut around each piece, one hole outside of stitching.

3. With black thread knotted at one end, go through body from front to back at point indicated, then through top of leg. Knot at back. Repeat with remaining leg. Thread cord through top of each leg and tie them together. Cut a 5-inch (13cm) length of cord for pull cord and tie to center of cord, connecting legs and letting loose end hang below body. Tie small bead to end of pull cord. Cut another length of cord and thread through top of rooster for hanger.

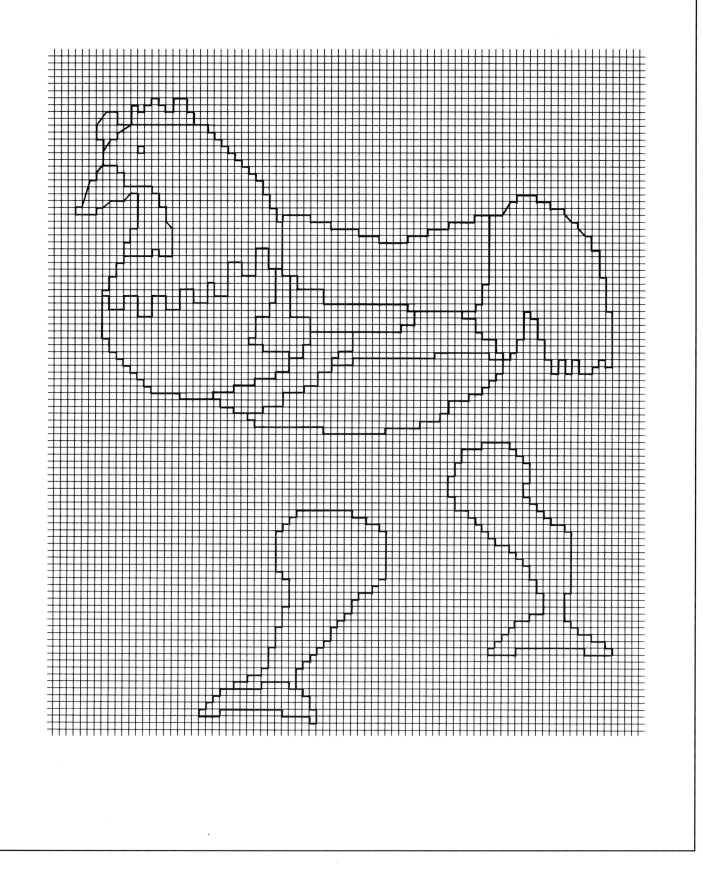

Peacock

MATERIALS

- Scraps of teal or turquoise felt
- Thread to closely match felt
- Small amount of Fiberfil stuffing
- Three feathers to match felt, approximately 3 inches (7.5cm) long
- Fine glitter in opalescent, turquoise, and teal
- Glue
- Small piece of 24-gauge craft wire
- Small spring clothespin, approximately 1¾ inches (4.5cm) long, painted dark green
- Black and brown paint

The bright turquoise and teal glitter, which make up the spectacular eyes markings on the tail of this peacock's plumage, will add a marvelous sparkle to your holiday decorations.

I. Using the full-size patterns provided below, cut two bodies and one insert from felt. Holding body pieces together and using matching thread, sew a tiny overcast stitch along the top neck edge and around the beak to the point where the insert joins. Sew along one edge of insert then return to beginning of insert, and sew along other edge to the tail. Return to the top back of neck edge and sew remaining portion of back seam, stuffing body with Fiberfil as you close the seam.

2. With a small brush, paint an oval of glue of approximately ⅞ inch (2cm) long on largest feather, and ⅝ inch (1.5cm) on smaller feathers. Dust glued areas with teal glitter. When glitter has dried, shake off excess and

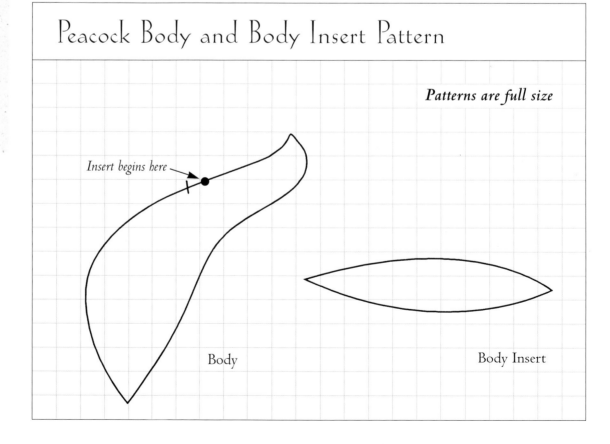

Peacock Body and Body Insert Pattern

Patterns are full size

Insert begins here

Body

Body Insert

paint a smaller oval of glue in the center of the teal oval and dust with turquoise glitter. Shake off excess. Touch edges of feather lightly with glue and dust with opalescent glitter. Shake off excess.

3. With black paint and a pin, paint a small eye on either side of head. Paint beak brown.

4. With scissors, poke a small hole in center of peacock's back about ½ inch (1.25cm) below base of neck. Glue end of larger feather into hole. Repeat the procedure with remaining smaller feathers, gluing one to each side and placing it slightly back from the center feather. Glue peacock to clothespin.

5. Cut three 1½-inch (4cm) lengths of craft wire. Coat end of each lightly with glue and roll in turquoise glitter. Let dry. Dip glitter-coated ends in glue and lightly dust the bead of glue with the same glitter. Let dry thoroughly. Cut glitter-trimmed wires to ¼ to ³⁄₈ inch (6mm to 1cm) in length. Poke a small hole in top of peacock's head and glue wires in place for head ornament.

Rocking Rabbit

MATERIALS

* Terra-cotta cookie mold (this one is Rocking Rabbit from Brown Bag Cookie Art; see Sources on page 116)
* Natural beeswax (available from Cookie Art Exchange; see Sources on page 116)
* Microwave-safe bowl or container
* Vegetable oil
* Acrylic paints
* Satin finish sealer
* Ribbon for hanging
* Microwave oven
* Oven mitts
* Small sharp knife

Another whimsical cookie mold, this time filled with wax, yielded this charming ornament.

>—+—◆◆—O—◆◆—+—<

1. Put mold in refrigerator for 20 minutes.

2. Place wax in microwave-safe bowl (preferably a disposable one), and microwave at medium setting, checking progress frequently. Wax should just melt, not boil.

3. Remove mold from refrigerator and coat lightly with vegetable oil. Holding container with oven mitts, pour wax quickly into mold, filling it up to edge of detail. Let mold cool and wax harden; it will shrink away from the edges as it cools.

4. Remove wax from mold and trim with knife if necessary. (I also cut out the area inside the rocker). You can use your fingernail to adjust modeling around edges, if desired.

5. When wax is completely cool, paint as desired with acrylic paints or follow my example in the photograph on the opposite page. Finish with two or more coats of satin finish sealer, following manufacturer's directions.

6. To attach hanging ribbon, heat blade of knife in hot water or in direct flame and press knife to back of ornament to soften wax. Place ribbon on soft spot and press to secure with hot knife.

Sheep

MATERIALS

- Small piece of white fake fur
- Small amount of Fiberfil stuffing (optional)
- Chenille stem
- Small piece of black felt
- Matching thread
- Cord for hanging

A vacation in rural Ireland provided the inspiration for these cuddly ornaments sewn, quite simply, of fake fur and felt.

⇥━◆━━O━━◆━⇤

1. Trace patterns on the next page and cut two body pieces from fake fur, taking care to reverse pattern when cutting the second piece. From black felt, cut four legs, two head pieces, and two ear pieces.

2. Cut chenille stem into four 1½-inch (4cm) lengths. Place one chenille stem on one felt leg piece, positioning end of stem in center of rounded portion. Using black thread, stitch edges together tightly around the chenille stem, working from the top down. When approximately ¼ inch (6mm) from bottom, fold up remaining felt and stitch tightly together to create a hoof. Before cutting thread, wrap tightly around top of hoof and knot. Repeat with remaining chenille stem and felt pieces.

Sheep Body Patterns

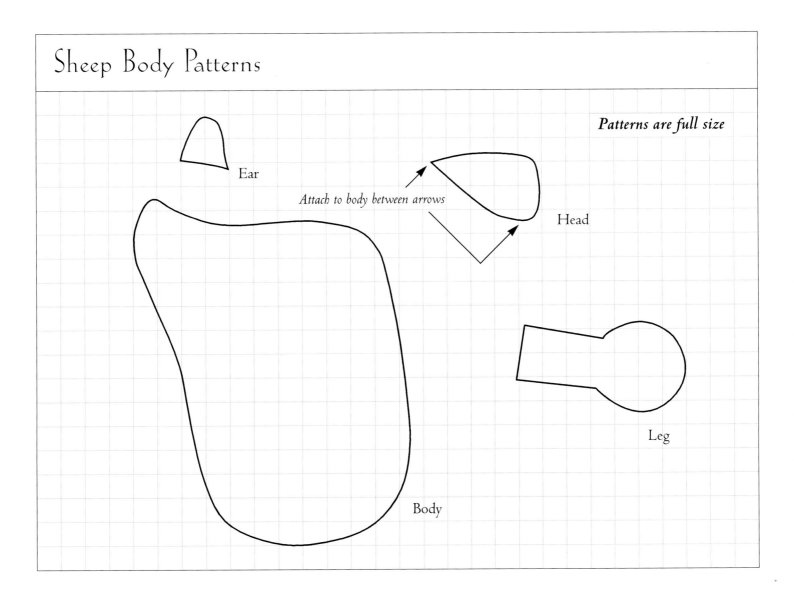

Ear

Patterns are full size

Attach to body between arrows

Head

Leg

Body

3. With white thread, use an overcast stitch to sew body pieces together, wrong sides together, from crown of head, along back, and down to base of body. Change to black thread and stitch around front and bottom edges of black felt head pieces. Position head against body and stitch in place along both sides using black thread and the same small overcast stitches. When possible, hide the stitches in the fur. With white thread, resume stitching the body seam below the head to the base of body. As you stitch along the base of sheep, insert legs and stitch in place as you go. Before closing body seam, stuff lightly with Fiberfil, if desired. Fold and glue one corner of each ear toward center. Glue ears in place to top of head. Tack a loop of cord to top of sheep for hanging.

Squirrel

MATERIALS

➤ Brown felt

➤ Matching thread

➤ Fiberfil stuffing

➤ 1-by-4-inch (2.5 by 5cm) piece of brown fake fur

➤ Chenille stem

➤ Two small black beads for eyes

➤ Black thread or paint for nose

➤ Small acorn, painted gold

➤ Glue

The large population of squirrels that hang around my front door were the models for this ornament. A gold-painted acorn held between this squirrel's front paws is a special treat.

>—◆—○—◆—<

1. Trace squirrel body part patterns on the next page and cut from brown felt. You should have two bodies, four arms, four legs, two ears, one head insert, one body insert, two leg inserts, and two foot inserts.

2. Position head insert at point indicated on one body piece. From right side, use a very small overcast stitch to sew the two pieces together. Match second body piece to first and sew to insert along remaining edge. In same manner as head insert, stitch body

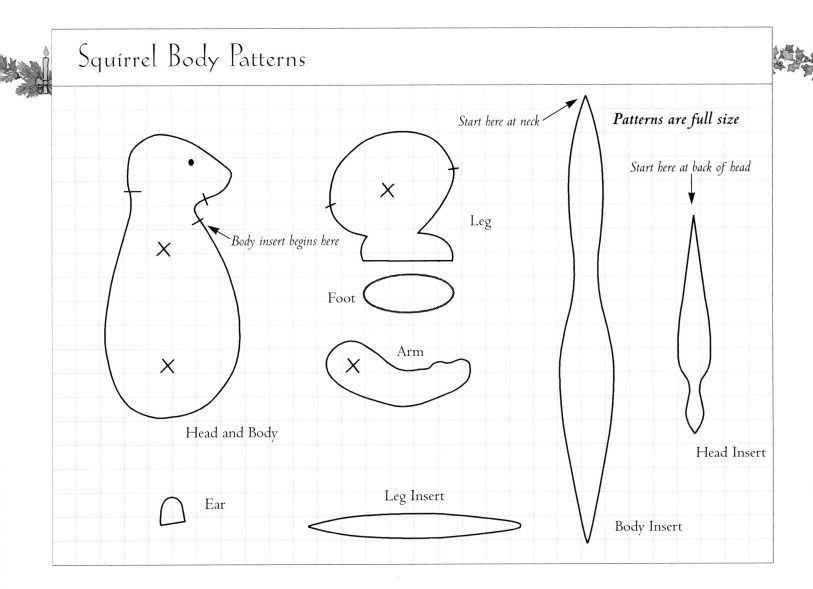

Start here at neck

Patterns are full size

Start here at back of head

Leg

Body insert begins here

Foot

Arm

Head and Body

Ear

Leg Insert

Body Insert

Head Insert

pieces together around nose and neck to the point where body insert is joined. Stitch remaining body seams, stuffing firmly with Fiberfil before closing.

3. Position leg insert at point indicated and stitch between leg pieces in same manner as body. Stitch remaining leg seams to base of foot. Position and stitch foot insert to base of foot, stuffing leg and foot moderately with Fiberfil before closing seam. Repeat for remaining leg and set aside. Holding two arm pieces together, stitch around edges using overcast stitch. Stuff lightly before closing seams. Repeat with remaining arm pieces. Glue legs and arms in position at points indicated to sides of body.

4. Lay chenille stem along center back of fur strip and tack in place at base, then, using an overcast stitch, sew the edges and top of the fur strip together, hiding the stitches in the fur. Bend the tail into shape and clip excess chenille stem 1/4 inch (6mm) beyond tail. Poke a small hole in back of squirrel and glue in base of tail.

5. Stitch one black bead to either side of head for eyes. With black thread or paint, make nose. Fold and glue one corner of each ear toward center and glue ears to top of squirrel's head. Glue gold acorn between paws. Stitch a loop of cord.

Chapter Four

Icons of the Season

Clay Santa from Chocolate Mold

MATERIALS

- Two-sided Santa chocolate mold with clips for holding halves together (see Sources on page 116)

- Air-drying clay (I used Model Magic by Crayola)

- Acrylic paints

- Small, sharp scissors or craft knife

- Sandpaper or emery board

- Satin finish sealer (optional)

- Eye pin

- Cord or ribbon for hanger

This Santa was made from a chocolate mold and lightweight air-drying clay painted for a most charming effect.

1. Open chocolate mold and press a thick layer of clay into each half, pushing clay into all the details until it reaches the top of the mold. Fit the two halves together, squeezing as tightly as possible to seal the edges together. Clamp and allow to dry, following clay manufacturer's directions.

2. When clay has cured, carefully open the mold and remove the figure. Set piece aside to dry completely. With scissors or craft knife, trim any excess clay protruding from the sides of the figure, then use the sandpaper or emery board to smooth the seam lines.

3. Paint the figure as desired, following the details of the mold and the picture on the next page as a guide. Finish with a coat of satin finish sealer, if desired.

4. With a needle or pin, make a guide hole in top of figure. Trim the eye pin to 1/2 inch (1.25cm) if necessary, and glue into prepared hole. Tie a cord or ribbon through the eye pin to make hanger.

Paper Santa from Chocolate Mold

MATERIALS

- Two-sided Santa chocolate mold with clips for holding halves together (see Sources on page 116)

- Red construction paper

- Small amount of cotton linter (short fiber cotton pulp paper for paper making/casting)

- Blender

- Sieve

- Sponge

- Vegetable oil

- Glue

- Fine white opalescent glitter

- White paint

- Fine sandpaper or emery board (optional)

- Eye pin

A paper Santa ornament cast in a chocolate mold is trimmed in utter simplicity with white glitter making an all-time classic ornament.

⊰━┾◆┾━◦─O─◦━┽◆┽━┾

1. Apply a light coating of oil to inside of chocolate mold halves, wiping away excess.

2. Tear construction paper and linter into small pieces and place in blender container with a quart of water. Let paper soak for about 20 minutes. Blend mixture with short bursts until reduced to pulp. Turn pulp into sieve and allow to drain until water drips.

3. Press a thick layer of pulp into each half of mold, making sure the pulp rises slightly above the mold edges so that when pressed together, the two halves will join. Use sponge to remove all excess water before pressing the two halves of the mold together and fastening with clips. With your finger, reach through the open bottom of the mold to press edges together. Set mold aside for several days to dry.

4. When mold feels fairly dry, remove clips and very carefully remove casting. If it is sticking or pulling apart, remold and let dry longer. If upon removal the two halves separate, allow them to dry completely, then match and glue the edges together. Trim edges, sanding lightly if necessary.

5. Working with one area at a time, quickly and carefully brush white paint over surfaces, such as beard, hat, coat, or sleeve trim, where glitter will be applied. Holding figure over paper, quickly sprinkle glitter over wet surface. Shake excess glitter onto paper and return to container. Continue to apply paint and glitter as desired.

6. Use a pin or needle to make a guide hole at top of figure. Trim eye pin, if necessary, and glue into prepared hole. Thread with cord for hanging.

Clothespin Angel

MATERIALS

* Wooden, peg-type clothespin

* Two small wooden beads

* Chenille stem

* Acrylic paints

* Sandpaper or emery board

* Scrap of burgundy satin

* Ivory lace, approximately 3 inches (7.5cm) wide with scalloped border

* Assorted gold braids, as desired (see note)

* White glue

* Small amount of yellow roving for hair (curly yarn may be substituted)

* 5-inch (13cm) square of gold foil paper

An old-fashioned peg clothespin has been outfitted as an angel complete with gold foil wings and a halo of golden thread.

1. With sandpaper or emery board, sand top of clothespin, if necessary. Using the end of a paintbrush to create even, round dots, paint small black dots for eyes, medium dark pink dot for mouth, and larger, light pink dots for cheeks.

2. Trace pattern for skirt from the next page onto wrong side of burgundy satin. Run a thin line of glue along traced line to seal edges when cut. When glue is dry, cut out skirt.

Glue narrow gold trim around edge of skirt. Overlap center back edges by 1/8 inch (3mm) and glue together. Slip skirt over clothespin and glue in place, leaving approximately 1/8 inch (3mm) of clothespin showing below skirt. To form gathers in skirt, glue center front and back hem to clothespin at feet, and center point of each side to leg. Wrap and glue one or more lengths of plain gold braid around bodice to cover top of skirt to point where clothespin begins to curve in for neck.

3. Cut a 6-inch (15cm) length of lace. Glue edges of lace together to form tube. Gather top edge of tube, and position over skirt on clothespin, pulling up the stitches and gluing in place. Glue a length of decorative braid over top of lace gathers and another length around top of bodice.

4. Using pattern provided on the next page, cut two pieces of lace for sleeves. Fold under 1/8 inch (3mm) at bottom edge and glue in place. Roll sleeve around a pencil or pen, overlapping and gluing side seam. At cap of sleeve, pinch in sides, fold over top 1/8 to 1/4 inch (3 to 6mm) and glue in place. Cut two 1 1/8-inch (4cm) lengths of chenille stem and glue one end of each into wooden beads. Glue opposite ends inside sleeves, and glue sleeves to sides of clothespin at shoulders.

5. Wrap and glue roving around head for hair. Cut a 2-inch (5cm) length of gold cord and form into a circle, gluing both ends to back of head for halo.

Clothespin Angel Dress and Wing Patterns

Patterns are full size

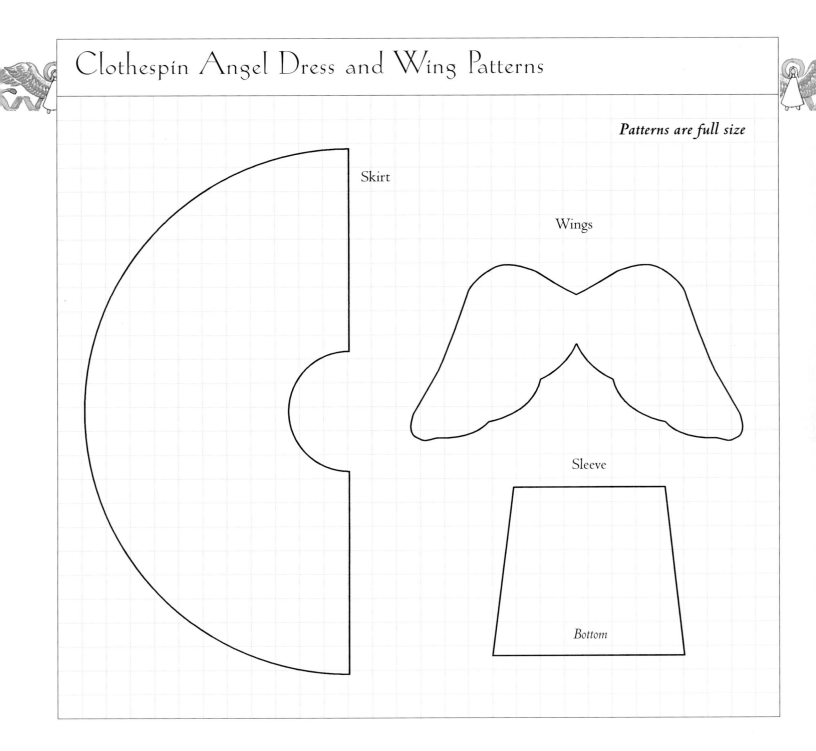

Skirt

Wings

Sleeve

Bottom

6. Fold gold paper in half and glue wrong sides together. Trace wing pattern to gold paper and cut out. Glue gold braid around edges of wings. Cut an 8-inch (20.5cm) length of gold cord and glue both ends to back of angel for hanger. Glue wing assembly to back of angel over ends of cord.

NOTE

I used a very narrow gold braid picot around the skirt, a flat braid for the bodice, a scalloped braid for bodice and wing trim, and a fine cable for the halo.

and feet according to diagram. Wrap center of remaining chenille stem around neck (below bead/head) and shape arms according to diagram on page the next, clipping off any excess.

4. Trace patterns on page 69 for hat, cape, and coat, and cut from natural batting, placing dotted lines on fold as indicated. In addition, cut two 1½-inch (4cm) squares for sleeves and four 1-by-½-inch (2.5 by 1.25cm) pieces for coverings for hands and feet. Clip a small piece of scrap batting and use it to pad feet.

5. For foot, wrap one of the covering pieces around the scrap and chenille stem, and stitch edges together in the back. Repeat on remaining foot. Do not pad hands with scrap, but cover them in the same manner as feet.

6. Place figure on wrong side of coat piece, folding the edges up and overlapping at front of figure. Glue edges together and glue top of coat to chenille stem. Wrap one sleeve piece over each arm, overlapping by approximately ⅛ inch (3mm) and slipstitch edges together with seam on inside of the arm. Cut tea-dyed batting into ⅜-inch-wide (1cm) strips. Glue one strip around bottom of coat and up the center front seam. Glue a strip around each sleeve cuff. With right sides of cape piece together and using a very narrow seam, stitch outer ½ inch (1.25cm) of shoulder seam on each side, leaving approximately ⅛ inch (3mm) open at center for neck. Turn cape right side out and glue tea-dyed strip around bottom and along one center front edge. Position cape around shoulders of figure, gluing side with trim over opposite side.

Cotton Batting Santa

MATERIALS

- 9-inch (23cm) square of unbleached cotton batting
- Brewed coffee or tea
- Two long chenille stems
- Wooden bead, ⅝ inch (1.5cm) in diameter
- Santa face scrap art
- Glue
- Toothpick
- Brown marker
- Small piece green tissue paper
- Small scrap of brown fabric
- Thread and needle
- Gold cord

This old-fashioned Santa, with his tea-dyed trim and tissue paper tree, harkens back to the days when many Christmas tree ornaments were made from cotton batting.

>─┤◆├─○─◆├─┤<

1. Cut a 2-inch (5cm) strip of batting and soak in coffee or tea until noticeably darker than remaining batting. Rinse and set aside to dry.

2. Cut excess paper from around Santa face, clipping to edge of beard around the bottom and leaving some excess along the top edge, if possible, in order to have something to glue the cap to.

3. Thread wooden bead on one end of chenille stem, folding stem back on itself to hold bead in place. Fold remaining stem into legs

Cotton Batting Santa Patterns and Wiring diagram

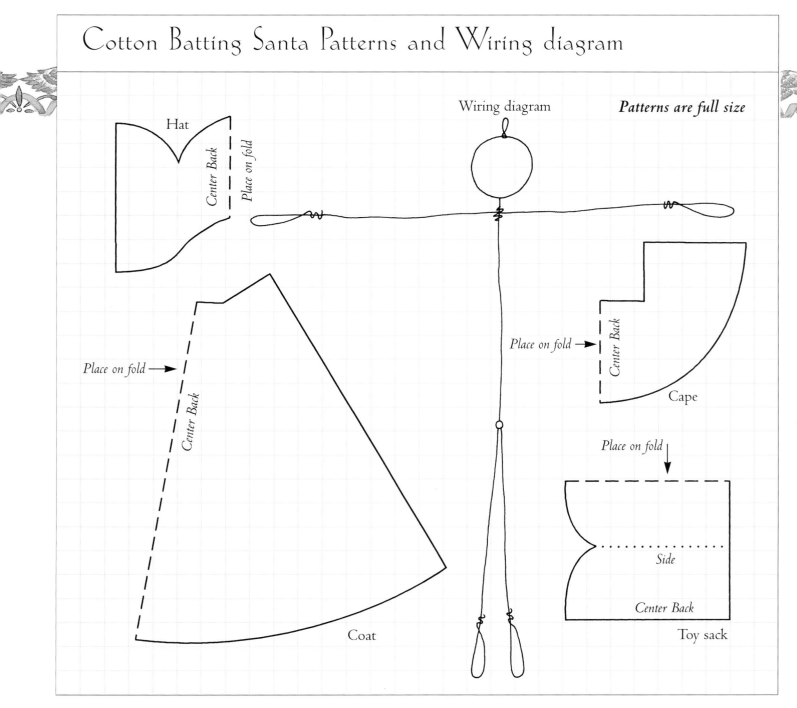

Hat — Center Back — Place on fold

Wiring diagram

Patterns are full size

Place on fold → Center Back

Cape

Place on fold ↓

Side

Center Back

Toy sack

Place on fold →

Center Back

Coat

7. Glue face cutout to front of wooden bead. With right sides together and using a narrow seam, sew center back seam of cap and then sew across the top. Turn right side out and glue to figure's head over the top edge of scrap face. Glue tea-dyed trim over bottom edge of cap.

8. Use marker to color toothpick brown. Cut three 1½-by-2-inch (4 by 5cm) pieces of green tissue paper. Glue one piece to one side of toothpick, and the remaining pieces, one on top of the other, on the reverse side of the toothpick, extending all three off the toothpick by about ¼ inch (6mm). Trim

tissue paper into tree shape. Fringe each side of tree shape. Rough up the edges a bit and place tree in Santa's arm. Trim end of tooth-pick and glue in place.

9. Trace pattern for sack and cut from brown fabric, placing dotted line on fold as indicated. With right sides together and using a narrow seam, sew side seam. Shift seam to center and sew across bottom of bag. Gather top edge of bag about ¼ inch (6mm) from edge and fasten off. Glue bag to coat, just below arm. Thread a piece of fine gold cord through back of hat for hanger.

Gold Crepe Paper Angel

MATERIALS

- 6-inch (15.5cm) square of gold metallic crepe paper
- 3/4 inch (2cm) diameter wooden bead or ball
- White paper doily
- 3 x 5 index card
- Thin gold cord for hair and hanger
- Purchased gold paper wings, 3½ inches (9cm) wide (available from D. Blumchen; see Sources on page 116)
- Black, dark and light pink, and red acrylic paints
- Glue
- Thread and needle
- Spray fixative or sealer

Gold crepe paper with its myriad of tiny folds makes a beautiful dress for this small angel ornament. Odds and ends of doilies complete her garments and gold thread her coiffure.

>—·<>·—·<>·—·<>·—·<

1. Paint wooden bead light pink. When dry, use the end of a paintbrush to paint two black dots for eyes, two larger, dark pink dots for cheeks, and a red dot for mouth. If desired, use a pin to draw out the paint at the sides of the mouth. Set aside to dry.

2. From gold crepe paper, cut one 3-by-6-inch (7.5 by 15cm) rectangle and two 1½-by-2-inch (4 by 5cm) rectangles with the paper crinkles parallel to the shorter dimensions. Fold under a ½-inch (1.25cm) hem along one long edge of larger rectangle. Overlap short ends by approximately ½ inch (1.25cm) and glue. Thread needle and knot end. Sew gathering stitches around top edge of crepe paper skirt. Pull up the gathers, leaving an opening at the top ⅛ to ¼ inch (3 to 6mm) across and fasten off the thread, securing it with a dot of glue. For sleeves, fold up ¼ inch (6mm) along one long edge of each of the smaller crepe paper rectangles. Overlap the short edges by ¼ inch (6mm) and glue. Gather the top edges same as for the skirt, except tighter, and fasten off the thread ends, securing them with glue.

3. Select a motif from paper doily to decorate the skirt and sleeve tops. Cut out carefully and glue in place. Glue sleeves to top of skirt. If desired, trim top of dress with a small piece of gold crepe paper or doily. Glue head to top of assembled dress.

4. Fold the index card in half. Wrap the gold cord 25 times around the shorter dimension. Tie the center of one side tightly with another piece of cord and clip the cord on the side opposite the tie. Glue cord to top of angel's head with strands hanging evenly over face and back of head. Trim bangs to just above eyes. Make a second bunch of hair in the same manner. Glue to top of head, side to side. Glue hair evenly around sides and back of head. Trim ends of hair to desired length. Glue wings to back of angel dress, placing underneath hair. For hanger, thread a length of cord through cord securing hair at top of head. Knot and trim ends, securing knot with drop of glue.

Kris Kringle

MATERIALS

- Terra-cotta cookie mold (this one is Kris Kringle 1996 from Brown Bag Cookie Art; see Sources on page 116)

- Cotton linter (short fiber cotton pulp paper for paper making/casting)

- Blender

- Sieve

- Cotton dish towel

- Clean sponge

- Microwave (optional, but extremely helpful)

- Acrylic paints

- Oven mitts

- Spray finish for sealer

- Glue and ribbon for hanger

Terra-cotta cookie molds help you to make beautiful ornaments for your tree or for decorating packages. Here paper pulp was shaped in a Santa mold and painted.

>+·+>·O·<+·<

1. Fill blender container about half full with water. Tear one sheet of linter into small pieces and add to the water. Let soak about 20 minutes. Blend mixture with short bursts until no visible pieces remain. It should look like cloudy white pulp suspended in water. If your blender is straining at all, add more water. Pour mixture into sieve and allow to drain until water drips slowly.

2. Scoop pulp up loosely and pat into mold. Make sure you have all areas of mold loosely covered with pulp before compressing it more firmly. Compress pulp into all details of mold, making sure you have an adequate, but not overly thick layer of fiber filling the entire mold and extending over the edges. When all fibers have been pressed into place, and as much remaining water as possible has been poured off, place mold on folded towel and use sponge to further press and absorb. Use a second folded towel to remove as much water as possible.

3. At this point, you can set the mold aside to dry overnight, or put it into the oven at 150°F (65° C) for 3 hours. Or, you can dry it in the microwave, placing it in the middle and setting the oven on full power for 1

minute. After 1 minute, rotate the mold one-half turn and set timer for 30-second intervals, rotating mold until paper is dry. Use oven mitts to handle mold as you turn and finally remove it from the oven. Use a thin-bladed knife to carefully lift edges of paper casting and peel it out of mold.

4. Paint paper casting with acrylic paints as desired. The paper casting is very absorbent, so work carefully, dabbing off excess moisture from brush before applying paint to paper. Also, take care not to work over the surface repeatedly in any one area since you will start to destroy the molded surface. Alternatively, you may use markers, colored pencils, or water colors to color your casting if you desire. When paint is dry, finish with a spray of clear finish and glue a loop of ribbon to the back for a hanger.

NOTE

Paper castings made by this method are rather absorbent and painting must be done carefully. Brown Bag Cookie Art makes a powder called Paper Clay (see Sources on page 116) that may be added to pulp in the blender to give the casting a harder finish. You may also try a spray of workable fixative available at most art supply stores to seal the surface and make decorating your paper casting a bit easier.

Nutcracker

MATERIALS

- ✦ Nutcracker hand press cookie mold (I used one from Brown Bag Cookie Art; see Sources on page 116)
- ✦ Salt dough (recipe at left)
- ✦ Acrylic paints
- ✦ Satin finish sealer
- ✦ Baking sheet
- ✦ Ribbon for hanger

All suited up in his dress blues and gold braid, this nutcracker medallion was created with a cookie stamp press and basic salt dough.

1. Form a 2-inch (5cm) ball of salt dough and flatten slightly between hands. Flour lightly on both sides and place on baking sheet. Lightly dust cookie stamp with flour and center over dough, flattening it with even pressure until dough extends a scant 1/4 inch (6mm) around edges of stamp. Lift stamp straight up and off dough. If it sticks, roll dough up and try again with a little more flour, dusting until a good impression is achieved. Trim edges of dough to approximately 1/4 inch (6mm) beyond design. Use a toothpick or pin to make a small hanging hole at top of design.

2. Preheat oven to 225°F (110°C). Bake ornament in center of oven for 30 minutes. Transfer directly to oven rack and bake for an additional 1 1/2 hours until dry and hard. Cool on rack.

3. When ornament is completely cool, paint as desired or according to the photograph and finish with two or more coats of satin finish sealer. Thread ribbon through hole for hanger.

SALT DOUGH RECIPE

2 cups (240g) flour, plus extra flour for dusting
1/2 cup (60g) salt
3/4 cup (100g) cold water

Mix flour and salt together, add the water, and stir until the flour is incorporated. Turn the dough onto a smooth surface and knead for about 5 minutes.

Burnt Brown Paper Snowman

This fun technique has transformed plain brown paper into a snowman with the texture of old metal. Twisted wire arms add to the effect.

>─┼─◆─○─◆─┼─<

NOTE

This project involves working with an open flame. Be cautious when crafting with children.

Structural paint by Liquitex is a new product that may be squeezed from the tube like icing, and hardens without flattening. It is used here to create the dimensional nose, eyes, mouth, and buttons. Thick white glue or modeling material may be substituted.

I. Trace pattern on next page twice to brown paper and cut out. Apply a fine line of glue just around the outside edge of one brown paper shape, leaving 2 inches (5cm) at bottom unglued. Place remaining brown paper shape on top and seal the glued edges.

2. Fold an 18-inch (46cm) length of craft wire in half, twisting ends together. Spread a thick layer of glue on one side of snowman shape. Light the candle and leave it burning on a safe surface. Slip the twisted wire inside the snowman and hold glued side over candle flame so that the surface bubbles and blackens. If you get any little flare-ups, blow them out immediately. The goal is to get the entire surface blackened with a bubbly texture. Let snowman cool. With fingers or tissue,

lightly rub surface to remove excess soot and to achieve maximum texture. Apply glue to remaining side of snowman and repeat the procedure. Set snowman aside until glue is thoroughly dry and surface has lost all stickiness.

3. Remove wire and lightly stuff snowman with Fiberfil and glue bottom opening closed.

4. Using a small piece of sponge, crumpled tissue, or your fingers, apply white paint to front and back of snowman, taking care not to fill in all the texture and leaving some light and dark areas.

5. With a plain round-holed tip on the tube of structural paint, work a triangular, "carrot" nose, irregular "rock" eyes, mouth, and buttons on front of snowman. Let dry. Paint eyes and buttons black and carrot nose orange.

6. Fold and twist 8-inch (20cm) lengths of wire into arms. With sharp scissors, poke starter holes on either side of snowman for arms. Insert and glue arms into position. Poke another hole at top back of head, inserting and gluing screw eye for hanging.

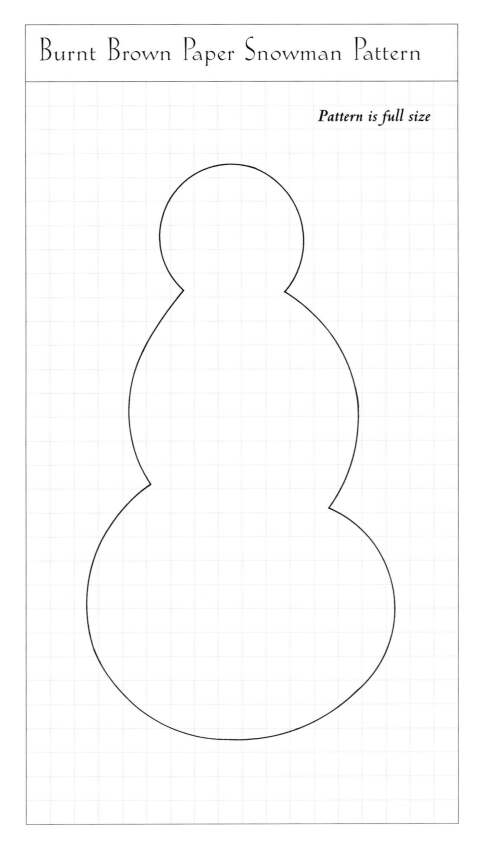

Burnt Brown Paper Snowman Pattern

Pattern is full size

Wiggle Snowman

MATERIALS

* Lightweight air-drying clay (I used Model Magic by Crayola)
* Acrylic paints
* White or light-colored sand
* Sparkle varnish
* 20-gauge craft wire
* Scissors or nippers for cutting wire
* Needle-nose pliers
* Strong glue for adhering wire to clay (I used a jewelry glue)
* Scrap of red fabric
* Scraps of gold metallic paper trims
* Structural paint by Liquitex (may substitute clay if desired) See note on page 76 about structural paint by Liquitex.
* Cord for hanging

This snowman wiggles when you touch him! Textured paint and a perky red cap add to his jaunty appeal.

⊱—┃—◆—┣—○—┫—◆—┃—⊰

1. Shape three balls of clay in graduated sizes for head and body of snowman. It is not necessary to make them perfectly round or smooth, since the sand paint will hide irregularities. With wire, poke guide holes in bottom of head ball, top and bottom of middle ball, and top of bottom ball. With a small piece of clay, shape a tiny carrot for nose. Set balls and nose aside to dry completely.

2. Mix sand with white paint and daub onto dry balls. Set aside to dry. If you did not use white sand, it may be necessary to paint sand-covered balls with an additional layer or two of white paint. Coat finished balls with sparkle varnish.

3. With scissors or nippers, cut four 1-inch (2.5cm) lengths of wire. With needle-nose pliers, bend a tight loop in one end of each piece. Thread loops together in sets of two and tighten to prevent loops from coming apart. Glue straight ends into starter holes made earlier, linking balls together into snowman. Paint carrot nose orange and glue in place to head.

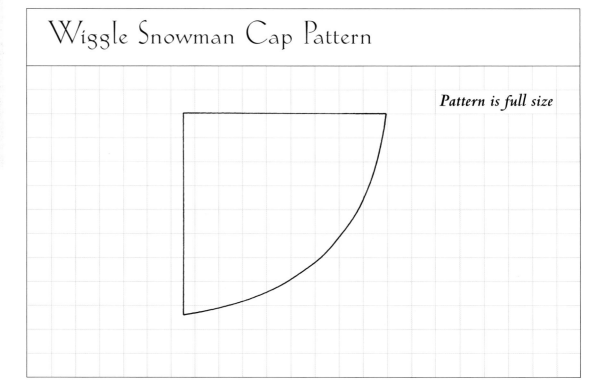

Wiggle Snowman Cap Pattern

Pattern is full size

4. With a plain round-hole tip on the tube of structural paint, work dots for eyes, mouth, and buttons. Check how balls hang to make sure buttons are properly aligned, and allow to dry. Paint eyes, mouth, and buttons black.

5. Trace cap pattern on the previous page and cut one from red fabric. With right sides together, stitch straight side seam. Turn cap right side out and tack to create a crumpled appearance. Glue cap to head. Cut and glue a bit of gold trim around hat edge.

6. Fashion a gold bowtie from other scraps of gold paper.

7. Trim and glue above top button. Tack a piece of cord to hat for hanging.

Parade of Toys

Carousel

MATERIALS

- Four assorted animal crackers
- Acrylic paints
- Satin finish sealer
- Brown Kraft paper
- ½-inch thick (1.25cm) sheet of Styrofoam
- Lightweight cardboard (I used a paper plate)
- White glue
- Hot glue gun
- Four toothpicks
- Small bead
- Gold metallic paper shelf trimming (I found this in a baking supply store. Similar trimmings are available from D. Blumchen; see Sources on page 116)
- Ribbon or cord for hanging

Fashioned from animal crackers, painted and varnished, and mounted on golden toothpicks, this carousel will reawaken fond memories of childhood.

1. Thin acrylic paint with water to achieve a more transparent look, and paint the front of each animal cracker. When crackers are completely dry, apply two coats of satin finish to front and back of each, allowing the first dry completely before applying the second. Set aside.

2. Trace circle pattern (on page 85) twice to foam sheet and three times to brown paper and cut out each. Use scrap foam to sand the edges of foam circles until they are flat and smooth.

3. From brown paper, cut two strips, one 1 inch by 12½ inches (2.5 by 31.5cm) and the other ¾ inch by 12½ inches (2 by 31.5cm). Apply glue to outside of one Styrofoam circle and center wider strip around the edge, with equal amounts of brown paper extending off top and bottom. When glue has set, clip extensions top and bottom every ¼ to ½ inch (6 to 15mm), folding and gluing these tabs to top and bottom of foam circle. Spread a thin layer of glue on one brown paper circle and glue over top of tabs on one side of foam circle. Trim any overhang. Repeat on opposite side of foam.

4. Trace carousel top pattern (on page 85) to lightweight cardboard and cut out. Spread a thin layer of white glue on one side and adhere to brown paper. Cut out leaving ¼ inch (6mm) extra brown paper along long curved edge. Clip small triangles from brown paper every ½ inch (1.25mm) along curved edge.

5. Roll up carousel top, overlapping edges until it fits snugly to top of remaining Styrofoam circle. Glue the overlapping edges. When glue has set, position top over foam circle and glue tabs to outer edge. Glue narrower strip of brown paper around edge over tabs, having one edge even with top edge of foam circle. Take care to leave no holes showing between strip and carousel top. Clip bottom of strip same as for carousel bottom, folding and gluing tabs to bottom of foam circle. Glue remaining brown paper circle to foam, covering tabs. Trim any overhang.

(Continued on page 84)

6. Cut a piece of lightweight cardboard 2¾ inch by 2 inch (7 by 5cm). Roll into a tube along the wider measurement, overlapping the ends by ¼ inch (6mm) and gluing (you should have a tube 2 inches [5cm] tall). Paint tube and carousel top and bottom as desired, or refer to photograph on previous page for guidance. When paint has dried, coat with two coats of satin sealer. Paint small bead and toothpicks gold.

7. From scrap paper cut out another circle the same size as carousel bottom. Fold it in quarters. Mark a point on each fold 1½ inch (4cm) from center. Center this pattern on carousel base and with one of the toothpicks poke a small starter hole at each location and also at center. Apply glue to base of tube and center over marked spot at center of carousel base. Put a small amount of glue on each toothpick and position one in each starter hole, sinking it approximately ¼ inch (6mm) into foam of base. Check to make sure each toothpick is as perpendicular as possible. Mark positions of toothpicks on base of carousel top same as for bottom, making the starter holes approximately ¼ inch (6mm) deep. Apply glue to top of tube and toothpicks and carefully lower top over bottom, lining toothpicks up with their guide holes and pressing the two together until center tube is resting against base of carousel top.

8. Using hot glue gun, apply a blob of glue to back of each animal and affix to toothpicks. Glue metallic paper trims to edges of carousel top and base. Glue small bead to peak of roof. Glue ends of hanging ribbon or cord inside bead.

Patterns are full size

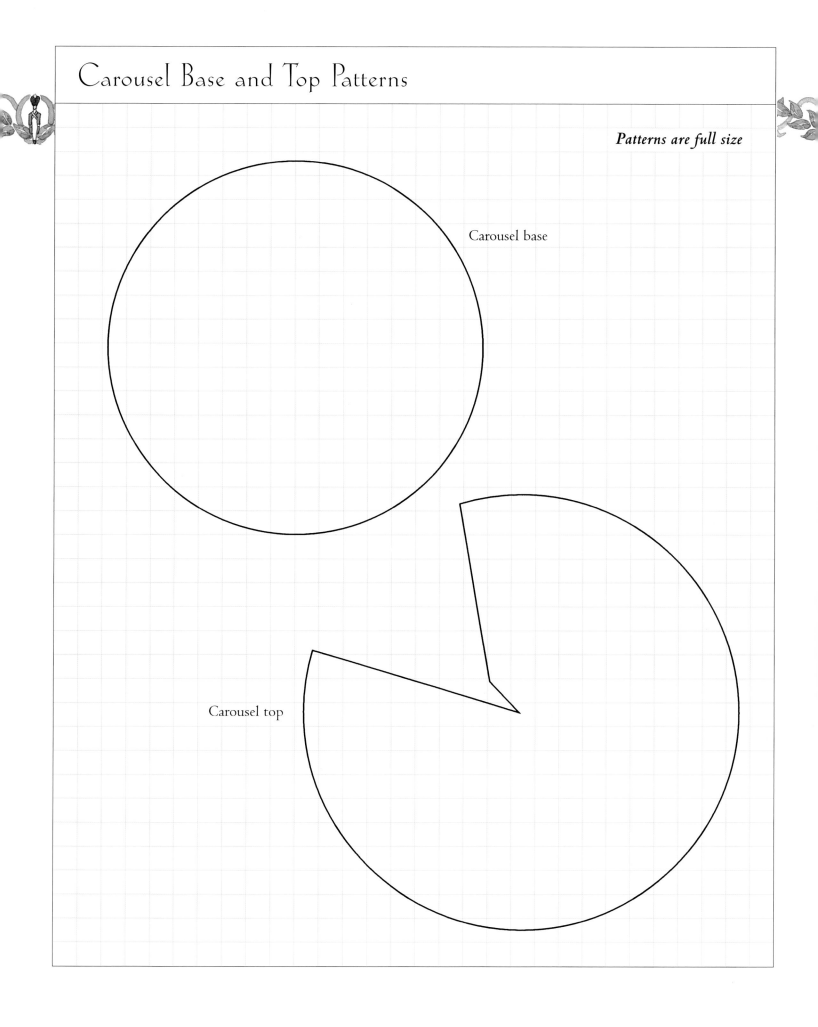

Carousel base

Carousel top

Musical Instruments

MATERIALS

ALL INSTRUMENTS:
- White tissue paper
- White glue

LUTE AND GUITAR:
- Small piece of ½-inch thick (1.5cm) Styrofoam
- Styrofoam ball, 2 inches (5cm) in diameter (Lute)
- Straight pins
- Acrylic paints
- Fine gold thread
- Gold metallic paint in squeeze applicator
- 7 inches (17.5cm) of ¼-inch (6mm) wide gold braid
- Sharp knife or small saw (I used one marketed for carving pumpkins)
- Goldfoil paper trims (Lute)
- Clear spray finish (optional)

DRUM:
- Medium-weight cardboard
- Small pieces of red and blue metallic papers
- ¼-inch (6mm) wide gold braid
- Two wooden matches
- Emery board or small piece of sandpaper
- Gold paint

All of these delightful miniature instruments were fashioned from Styrofoam and tissue paper. With their bright colors and gold accents, they look almost playable!

><->-O-<->-<

GUITAR

1. Trace and cut out patterns below for guitar body and neck. Place patterns on foam and mark around outer edges. Use small saw or knife to cut around body and neck, then to trim neck down as shown in the side view.

Use a scrap piece of foam to sand edges of guitar body and neck. Glue neck to top of body and reinforce with straight pin through back of neck into body. Allow to dry.

2. Tear white tissue paper into small pieces no larger than ½ inch by 1 inch (1.25 by 2.5cm). Thin glue with water. Using paintbrush, apply glue solution to guitar alternately with layers of tissue paper, smoothing the tissue paper on and around edges with the diluted glue until several layers have been applied over entire surface. Set aside to dry completely.

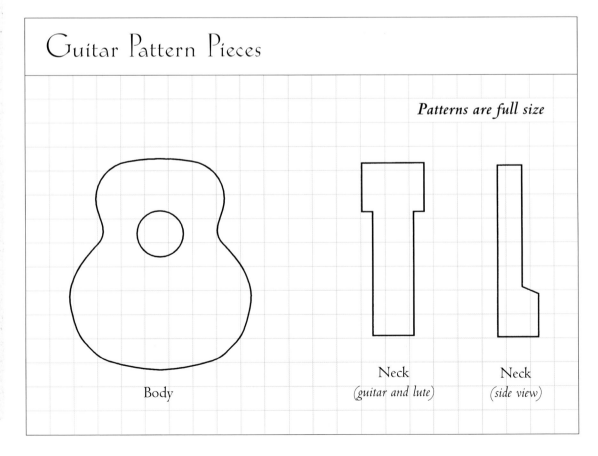

Guitar Pattern Pieces

Patterns are full size

Body

Neck
(guitar and lute)

Neck
(side view)

3. Paint guitar body, sides, and back of neck red. On guitar front, mark neck extension, hole, and bridge below hole, and paint black. With gold paint in squeeze applicator, paint frets (stripes) on the neck of guitar. With paintbrush and gold paint, paint around outside of guitar body and around hole. Spray with clear finish if desired. See above photograph for reference.

4. For strings, cut four 4-inch (10cm) lengths of gold thread. Glue one end of each string to bridge on guitar body. When glue has dried, draw each thread up along neck and glue to top, referring to photograph as necessary. When glue has dried, apply a dot of gold paint over each end of thread. Glue ends of gold braid to each end of guitar. When glue has dried, apply a dot of gold paint over glue.

LUTE

1. Trace and cut out patterns on pages 86 and 88. Cut Styrofoam ball in half and trace body pattern on flat side of ones half. Use small saw or knife to cut around pattern, and sand into pear shape. Cut away back portion of neck as indicated on side view and sand edges with a scrap piece of foam to neaten. Glue bottom of neck to top of pear-shaped base. Push one or two straight pins through neck base into body of lute to reinforce.

2. Tear tissue paper into small pieces and apply to lute with diluted white glue in same manner as guitar.

3. When lute is dry, paint purple. Mark and paint neck extension, hole and bridge same as for guitar. Outline lute body and edge of

hole with gold paint. If desired, work squiggly lines on back of lute body with gold paint. At this point, you may spray with clear sealer if desired. With gold paint in squeeze applicator, work fret lines randomly on neck of lute and set aside to dry. See photograph on page 87 for reference.

4. Cut four 6-inch (15cm) lengths of gold thread. Glue threads to lute same as for guitar, covering glue with gold paint when dry. Decorate front of lute with gold paper cutouts, as desired. Glue one end of gold braid to base of lute, opposite end to top. Cover ends of braid with gold paint in same manner as guitar. See photograph on page 87 for reference.

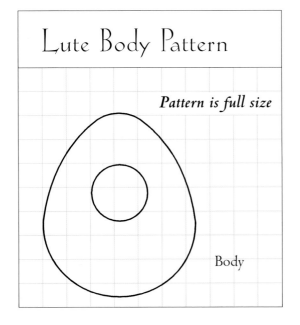

Lute Body Pattern

Pattern is full size

Body

1. Measure and cut one each from cardboard and red metallic paper a 1½-by-5½-inch (4 by 14cm) rectangle. Roll cardboard rectangle into a tube, overlapping ends by ¼ inch (6mm), and glue. Spread a thin layer of glue on back of red rectangle and cover tube.

2. Trace triangle pattern on this page to cardboard and cut out. Use cardboard pattern to mark triangle pattern six times on wrong side of blue metallic paper and cut out. Apply a thin layer of glue to backs of triangles and apply to drum, beginning at back seam and working around to front with next triangle just touching previous triangle at upper corner. Points of triangles should just reach bottom of drum. See photograph on page 87 for reference.

3. Cut four squares of tissue paper slightly larger than base of drum. Apply a thin bead of glue around base of drum and smooth one sheet of tissue paper over end. Place another bead of glue over the first and repeat with a second sheet of tissue paper. Both sheets should be taut with no ripples. Mix a small amount of white glue with water and brush over tissue paper inside rim of drum. Set aside to dry. The glue should pull the paper taught as it dries and leave it slightly shiny. When one end is dry, turn drum over and repeat procedure on opposite end. When both ends are covered, leave as is or paint white or ivory and finish with satin sealer. Trim edges of tissue paper a scant $\frac{1}{8}$ inch (3mm) beyond edges of drum and fold down along drum sides. Cut a piece of braid approximately 8 inches (20.5cm) long for hanging loop. Fold braid in half and glue ends close to top of drum at back.

4. Cut two pieces of gold braid each about $5\frac{1}{2}$ inches (14cm) long. Apply glue to back of one piece of braid and wrap tightly around top edge of drum, covering edges of tissue paper and ends of hanging loop at back. Glue remaining piece of braid around opposite end of drum.

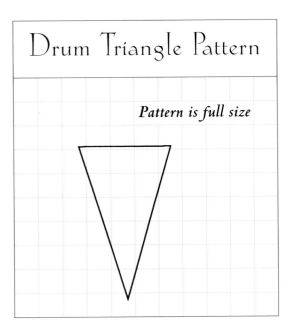

Drum Triangle Pattern

Pattern is full size

5. Light matches and extinguish as soon as chemicals have burned off. With sandpaper or emery board, sand off burned portion of match and round off sides and ends. Sand a drumstick head into one end of each match stick by sanding a gentle depression $\frac{1}{4}$ inch (6mm) from end and rounding off the edges. Paint drumsticks gold and glue across top of drum.

NOTE

This project involves working with an open flame.
Be cautious when crafting with children.

Pull Toys

MATERIALS

- Wooden animal cutout, approximately 2½ inches (6cm) long and ⅜ inch (1cm) thick (I used cutouts from Cherry Tree Toys; see Sources on page 116)
- Acrylic paints
- Crackle medium (optional)
- Sponge for painting (optional)
- Satin finish sealer
- Wood for bases (basswood, 1 inch by ¼ inch [2.5 by 6mm])
- Craft saw or knife
- Sandpaper
- Glue
- ¾ inch (2cm) pewter wheels and threaded nails for attaching wheels to base (available from Cherry Tree Toys)
- Small screw eye for hanger
- Cord for hanging

Pre-cut wooden shapes and cast pewter wheels are the secret behind these easy-to-make pull toys that recall the days before "battery operated."

>—◆>—◇—<◆—<

NOTE

I found it helpful to drill a guide hole in top of toy to receive screw eye hanger and in base of toy to receive the threaded nail. I then attached the wheels by holding the threaded nail (already inserted through the wheel) with pliers and twisting it into the prepared hole.

1. Paint animal as desired with acrylic paints or refer to photograph at right for reference. If crackle finish is desired, paint animal first with a base coat, then apply crackle medium according to manufacturer's directions. When set, finish painting as desired.

2. Cut a length of basswood slightly longer that the animal for base of toy: base for cow is 3 inches (7.5cm) long; base for chicken is 2⅛ inches (5.5cm) long. Sand edges smooth and paint. Glue painted animal to base and set aside to dry. Finish with one or more coats of sealer.

3. Antique wheels by coating them with black paint, wiping paint off with a tissue and leaving traces of black behind in the recessed areas. Attach the wheels to the finished toy bodies, screwing the nail pegs into the base just back from either end. Twist a screw eye into the top of toy, checking for balance, and thread a cord through for hanging.

Spool Dolls

MATERIALS

* Odds and ends of wooden pieces, balls, spools, wheels, candle cups, and the like (frequently you can find bags of assorted wood pieces in craft stores. Try to find balls for the heads with pre-drilled holes, otherwise hole will have to be drilled later to insert a hanging cord)

* Thick and tacky glue suited for wood

* Sandpaper (optional)

* Assorted acrylic paints

* Satin finish sealer

* Cord for hangers

Scraps of wooden turnings can, with a little imagination and paint, be turned into charming ornaments. Here they've been transformed into small doll ornaments.

>·I·>·O·<·I·<

1. Check wooden pieces for smoothness, sanding any rough spots if necessary. Glue the wooden pieces together into doll shape, taking care that hole in head ball is on top. Allow glue to dry.

2. Paint as desired or follow photograph on previous page. Make small circles for polka dots and eyes by using the handle tip of the paintbrush or the eraser of a pencil. Mouth can be painted with a fine brush or drawn with a thin marker. When all paint has dried, apply one or two coats of finish according to manufacturer's directions. Glue both ends of a 6-inch (15cm) length of cord into hole at top of doll head for hanger.

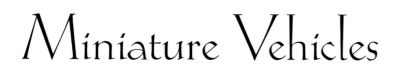

Miniature Vehicles

MATERIALS

- Styrofoam eggs: 2¾ inches (7cm) long for submarine; 3¼ inches (8cm) long for rocket ship
- Foam ball, 2 inches (5cm) in diameter for spaceship
- 3-inch (7.5cm) square of ½-inch thick (1.25cm) foam for spaceship
- Gesso
- Sandpaper
- Air-drying clay (conning tower and periscope for submarine)
- Acrylic paints
- Paintbrush
- Lightweight cardboard (I used an index card)
- Glue
- Sturdy nylon thread (hanger for submarine)
- Eye pins (hangers for rocket and spaceship)
- Toothpicks and small wooden beads (four of each for legs and feet of spaceship)
- Spray sealer
- Sharp knife or small saw (I used one marketed for carving pumpkins)

These fanciful vehicles made from simple Styrofoam shapes were painted in bold, bright colors and will appear to soar from the branches of your tree.

>+·+‹›·O·‹›·+‹

NOTE

When it comes to painting these little ornaments, look around for things that can make the job easier. Small dots of color can easily be applied with the end of a paintbrush or toothpick. Larger dots can be made with a pencil eraser, and so on.

SUBMARINE

1. Roll Styrofoam egg between hands to create a more uniform oval, flattening one end at the same time for the rear of the submarine. Paint submarine with several coats of gesso, letting each dry and sanding smooth before applying the next. A reasonably smooth surface should be achieved.

2. Shape a small piece of air-drying clay into a ball of approximately ½ inch (1.25cm) in diameter. Flatten ball into an oval and square off the sides and bottom. Position on top of submarine for conning tower. Smooth area where tower joins sub for best adhesion. With point of pen or end of paintbrush, poke a small hole on top to receive periscope. With another piece of clay, roll a small cylinder and cut to approximately ¾ inch (2cm) long. Bend top over at a right

angle to make periscope. Set aside periscope and sub with tower to dry. When dry, check to see if tower holds firmly to sub; glue if necessary and then glue periscope into prepared hole.

3. Using pattern provided below, cut two tail fin pieces from lightweight cardboard (I used two pieces of an index card glued together). Cut slits at center, from bottom of one fin and from the top of the other. Slip one fin over the other and into the slits just cut. Glue assembled fins to back of submarine. Paint tail and conning tower/periscope assembly with two coats of gesso, letting the first dry before adding the second.

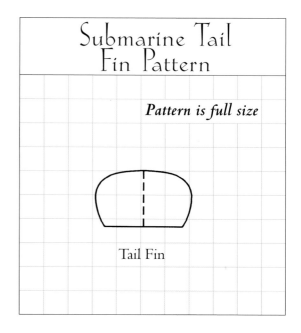

Submarine Tail Fin Pattern

Pattern is full size

Tail Fin

4. Give entire submarine two coats of paint (I used yellow), letting the first dry before adding the second. Paint rim of periscope black. Using a toothpick, add a row of black dots around top of conning tower. Using a new, flat pencil eraser, work three larger black dots along the center of each side of submarine. When black paint is dry, paint inside of periscope rim white, and add a light blue dot inside each large black dot on sub's side. Use above photograph for reference. Finish with a coat of spray sealer. Tie and glue a length of nylon thread around base of periscope for hanger.

3. Paint as desired or follow my example from photograph. I painted the body green and base, fins and flame details red. The nose cone was painted white and a ring of black dots was added around the base. I then created four windows with black paint surrounded by white and evenly spaced them around the body.

4. Trim an eye pin to approximately ½-inch (1.25cm) long. Poke a guide hole in top of rocket, apply glue to eye pin, and insert in prepared hole. Wipe off any excess glue. Spray completed rocket ship with two coats of sealer.

ROCKET SHIP

1. Roll and compress the Styrofoam egg between fingers and hands until a narrower egg shape of fairly dense foam has been achieved. See above photograph for desired shape. With a small saw or knife, cut the back end of rocket flat. Using the same process described in instructions for the submarine on page 94, coat the rocket with gesso. Let dry and sand smooth three times, or until you are satisfied with the texture of the surface.

2. Trace the rocket fin pattern at right to lightweight cardboard four times and cut out. Make any necessary adjustments on the inner angle of the fins so that they fit flush with the sides and bottom of the rocket, and then glue in place, spacing equidistantly around the rocket base. Apply another coat of gesso to the entire ship, including fins. Allow to dry, then sand smooth.

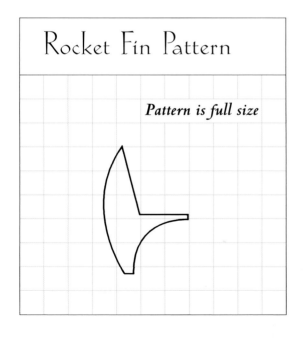

Rocket Fin Pattern

Pattern is full size

SPACESHIP

1. Trace a circle approximately 3 inches (7.5cm) in diameter onto $\frac{1}{2}$-inch thick (1.25cm) piece of foam, using any bottle or other round object that comes close to that dimension as a guide. Cut out with sharp knife or small saw. Compress edges of disc, rounding them into an appropriate spaceship shape. See photograph for reference. Roll and compress the ball in the same manner as the submarine and rocket ship (see pages 94–96). Cut the compressed ball in half. Glue one half of the ball on top of the disc and, when the glue has dried, coat the assembled spaceship body with gesso and sand as before.

2. When you are satisfied with the surface texture, paint as desired or follow my example. I painted the body orange and the ring blue. As with the previous two ships, I worked a ring of black dots around the top and created four white windows outlined in black for the body. Refer to photograph for reference.

3. Glue a wooden bead to the end of each toothpick, sliding the bead up the toothpick and trimming off the pointed end. Paint the leg assemblies. Trim the assembled legs to 1 inch (2.5cm). Mark bottom of disc at four evenly spaced points for leg placement, and make a guide hole at each location. Apply glue to each leg and position in prepared holes, taking care that upper portion of leg goes into base at an angle toward the dome so it will not protrude from the disk.

4. Trim an eye pin to $\frac{1}{2}$ inch (1.25cm). Make a guide hole in the center top of the spaceship. Apply glue to the eye pin and place in prepared hole. Wipe away any excess glue. Spray completed spaceship with two coats of sealer.

Chapter Six

Visions of Sugar Plums

Bonbons

MATERIALS

- Cylindrical styrofoam, 1 inch (2.5cm) in diameter and 1 inch (2.5cm) in length for each bonbon

- Air-drying clay or bread dough (a slice of white bread without any crust torn up and mixed with 1 tablespoon of tacky white glue)

- White structural paint by Liquitex with leaf and star tips (for product information, refer to Burnt Brown Paper Snowman on page 76)

- Acrylic paints

- Gloss finish

- Small gold foil petit four cups

- Small gold eye pin and gold cord for hanger

They look like the sugarplums of Christmas dreams, but these sweets are actually made from bread dough disguised by paint and varnish, so they can decorate your tree for years to come.

>─I─◆>─◐─<◆>─I─◂

1. Cut a 1-inch (2.5cm) piece of the Styrofoam and round off one end by sanding with a scrap piece of foam.

2. Flatten a small ball of air-drying clay or bread dough by hand or with rolling pin into a circle of approximately 3 to 3½-inches (7.5 to 9cm) across. Place rounded end of foam piece in center of bread dough and draw edges up around foam, smoothing them flat across the bottom. It doesn't matter how well the bottom is finished, as it will be concealed inside the foil cups. Set covered foam aside to thoroughly dry.

3. Paint dry foam "bonbons" chocolate brown. When paint has dried, coat with one or more layers of gloss finish and allow to dry. Using a leaf tip on structural paint tube, form two leaves on top of each bonbon, placing one leaf on either side of center. Set aside to dry. When leaves have dried, use star tip to add a flower at the center of the two leaves. Allow to dry. When decorations have dried, use a fine brush to very carefully paint the leaves and flowers in pastel colors, as

desired or refer to photograph on next page for guidance. Test fit the bonbon in foil petit four cup. I found it necessary to trim ¼ inch (6mm) from the top of each cup for a more pleasing appearance. Glue bottom of bonbon inside of foil cup and, if necessary, glue sides of foil in place as well. With a needle, poke a guide hole just behind the pastel decoration on top of bonbon. Trim eye pin, if necessary, and glue into prepared hole. Thread gold cord through for hanger.

NOTE
One bonbon pictured was decorated with a plain round-holed tip that was used to create four loops, on top of which a star tip flower was added.

Christmas Crackers

Reminiscent of Victorian celebrations, these shining Christmas cracker ornaments belie their exceeding simple construction.

MATERIALS

- Cylindrical Styrofoam, 1 inch (2.5cm) in diameter and 2 inches (10cm) long for each ornament
- Foil papers, one piece (main color) approximately 3½ by 5½ inches (9 by 14cm) for each cracker, and two pieces in contrasting color for the fringe approximately 2 by 3½ inches (5 by 9cm)
- Assorted metallic paper trims, cut from doilies, shelf liner, and the like
- Glue
- Small eye pin
- Metallic cord for hanging

1. Cut a 2-inch (5cm) length of cylindrical foam, taking care to keep the ends straight.

2. Cut main and contrasting color foil pieces as indicated in Materials. Glue contrasting foil to the back of each end of larger piece of foil. When glue has dried, cut each end in ⅛-inch (3mm) fringe only to the depth of the contrasting foil. Spread a thin layer of glue on back of center portion, place foam piece in center, and wrap snugly around foam, sealing the edges. Twist foil at ends of foam, taking care not to rip off any fringe.

3. Cut a small scrap of contrasting foil, approximately ¼ inch (6mm) wide, and wrap and glue around twisted portion of foil close to ends of foam. Decorate as desired with scraps of contrasting foil and decorative elements cut from doilies or other materials. See photograph for a guide. Using a needle, poke a starter hole toward the end of foam section of cracker. Trim eye pin, if necessary, and glue into prepared hole. Thread cord through pin for hanger.

NOTE

One cracker pictured was covered with a crinkly gold metallic crepe paper. The main piece was cut 2 inches (5cm) longer and the excess on each end was folded under and glued. The ends were then left unfringed.

Clay Veggies

MATERIALS

⋆ Lightweight air-drying clay (I used Model Magic by Crayola)

⋆ Green tissue paper

⋆ Green floral wire

⋆ Acrylic paints

⋆ Glue

⋆ Spray sealer

⋆ Gold cord for hangers

An easy project for youngsters, these miniature vegetables are modelled from soft, air-drying clay, painted and finished with simple tissue paper leaves.

⋗━┥◆⟩━⊖━⟨◆┝━≺

CARROT

1. Form a piece of clay into a ball approximately 1½ inches (4cm) across. Roll and smooth clay until no seam lines show. Flatten ball between hands into a sausage, and then a cone, leaving it a bit lumpy for a more natural look. See photograph on next page for reference. Set aside to dry according to manufacturer's directions.

2. Paint dry carrot a light orange, and then add shades of orange for shading. When dry, spray lightly with sealer.

3. Cut four 5-inch (13cm) lengths of floral wire. Glue each length onto green tissue paper, approximately 1 inch (2.5cm) apart. Glue another piece of green tissue paper over wires. Trace leaf pattern on this page to lightweight cardboard and cut out. Center pattern over each tissue-covered wire and trace. Cut out leaves.

4. Cut an 8-inch (20cm) length of gold cord for hanger. Poke a hole in top of carrot and insert leaves and ends of gold cord. Glue in place. Fold over and arrange leaves as desired.

TOMATO

1. Form a piece of clay into a ball approximately 2 inches (5cm) across. Roll between hands until smooth and no seam lines show, flattening slightly for the somewhat squat tomato profile. With a knitting needle or pencil point, press a hole in top of tomato, then work lines of depression part way down tomato from top to mimic the rippled look of the top of a tomato. See photograph on next page for reference. Set aside to dry according to manufacturer's directions.

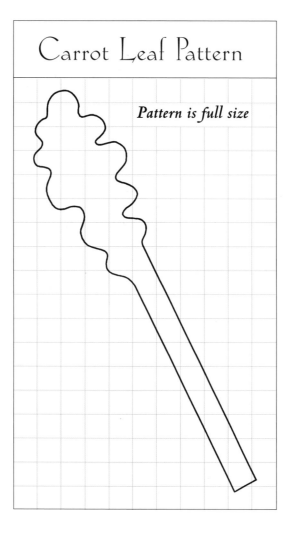

Carrot Leaf Pattern

Pattern is full size

2. When thoroughly dry, mix an orangey-red shade of acrylic paint and paint tomato. When dry, spray with sealer.

3. Trace tomato leaf pattern from this page onto green tissue paper and cut out. Cut a 3-inch (7.5cm) length of floral wire and fold in half, twisting the halves together. Fold in half, twisting the two halves together again.

4. Cut a 6-inch (15cm) length of gold cord for hanger. Apply glue to ends of cord and one end of wire stem, then insert all three into tomato. Crinkle the leaf and glue over stem, twisting around the stem and letting the remainder sit rather wrinkled at the top of the tomato.

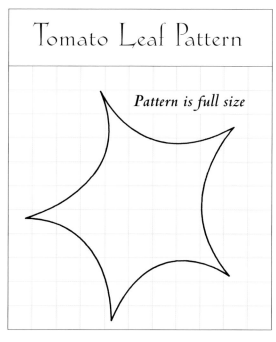

Tomato Leaf Pattern

Pattern is full size

Cotton Batting Fruit

Softly tinted and sparkling with glitter, these unusual fruit ornaments are reminiscent of the earliest Christmas tree ornaments, which were crafted of cotton batting.

>—+—◦—+—<

NOTE

These ornaments are designed with a very close-fitting skin of cotton batting over a foam base. General patterns are provided on the following pages for these skins, which are stretched and glued around their foam bases. As you stretch and shape the batting to the foam, you will have excess batting at the seam lines. Hold your scissors parallel to the foam base and cut off the excess batting, stretching and gluing the newly cut edges to meet as invisibly as possible. Try not to get any glue on the outside of the batting, since the paint will not cover the glue in the same way that it covers the batting.

When painting the cotton batting skins, it is necessary to start with the palest of colors and with the paint quite watered down. The batting absorbs the paint immediately and, while you can add succeeding layers of paint to darken the fruit, it is virtually impossible to lighten an area that is too dark.

PEAR

1. Roll foam egg between fingers and palms to create pear shape. The finished pear should be about ¼ inch (6mm) shorter than the original egg shape.

2. Fold batting in half, placing half pattern for pear skin on the next page on fold as indicated, and cut out. The batting cover is designed to fit very snugly. You will have to stretch it to cover the pear completely.

MATERIALS

* 3-inch (7.5cm) diameter Styrofoam egg for pear and lemon; 3-inch (7.5cm) diameter Styrofoam ball for peach

* 4-by-7-inch (10 by 18cm) scrap of cotton batting for each fruit

* Thick and tacky glue (the extra-thick glue doesn't soak into the batting as fast as a thinner glue might)

* Acrylic paints

* Spray glitter

* Artificial leaves

* Twig for peach and pear stems

* Gold cord for hangers

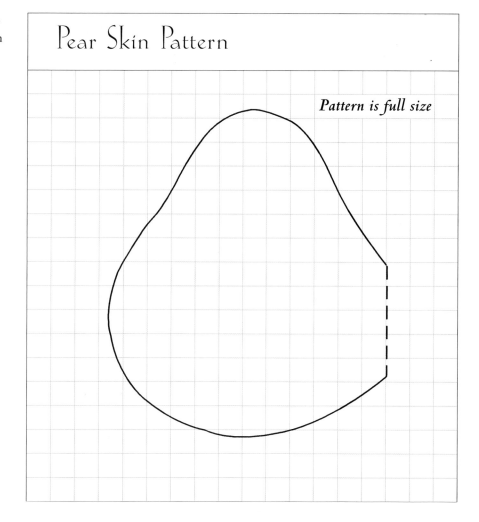

3. Spread a thin layer of glue around the fattest part of the foam pear, and then drape the cover over the glued area, following the note above for fitting the skin. Continue applying glue to remaining portions of the foam pear and stretch the batting to cover. As you work toward the top and bottom, cut away any excess folds of batting as described above. Strive to keep the joining seams as smooth and straight as possible. Rolling the covered pear between your hands will help to smooth out any lumpy spots. Set piece aside to dry.

4. Mix a pale shade of green paint for background color and apply to the entire pear. Make paint wet enough so it goes on lightly, but not so wet that it lifts the batting. When background color is dry, add shading to the pear with yellow, green, and pink as desired or refer to photograph as a guide. Lastly, with the end of the paintbrush, make an indentation at the top and bottom of the pear and paint indentations brown.

5. Insert a pin as a handle into the stem end of the pear. Spray with glitter. With sharp scissors, poke a hole in the top of the pear to receive the stem. Apply glue to the bottom of the stem twig and insert into the prepared hole. Glue leaf to top of pear. Tie or glue loop of gold cord to stem for hanger.

Pear Skin Pattern

Pattern is full size

PEACH

1. Roll 3-inch (7.5cm) foam ball between hands, compressing with fingers to condense the foam to a ball of approximately 2½ inches (6cm) across. With fingers or cap of a pen, make a small depression at top of peach. With a knitting needle or pencil point, make a shallow trench from top to center bottom for cleft on peach.

2. Place peach skin pattern from this page onto folded cotton batting and cut out in same manner as pear. Apply to peach, referring to directions for pear on page 107 if necessary. Set peach aside to dry.

3. With acrylic paints, mix a light peachy-orange and paint peach. When first coat is dry, apply additional layers to give peach the reddish blush and other tones that make it realistic. Refer to above photograph for a guide. Allow to dry, and then spray with glitter.

4. Poke a hole in the top with sharp scissors and glue stem and leaf in place. Tie or glue gold cord hanger to stem.

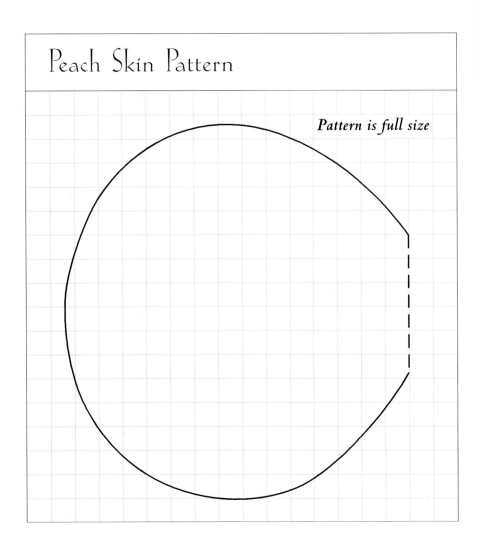

Peach Skin Pattern

Pattern is full size

brown to opposite end for blossom end of fruit. When paint has dried, spray with glitter.

4. Glue leaf to stem end of lemon. Glue loop of gold hanging cord in the same place, poking ends into fruit to hide.

LEMON

1. Roll and shape foam egg between hands and fingers until you achieve a satisfactory lemon shape.

2. Using pattern on this page, cut lemon skin from batting and apply to shape in same manner as pear (page 107).

3. When batting is dry, mix a diluted shade of light yellow acrylic paint, and paint lemon. When the first coat is dry, add additional shading as desired, referring to above photograph. With the end of a paintbrush, depress one end of lemon and paint brown, as if a stem had been there once. Add a dot of

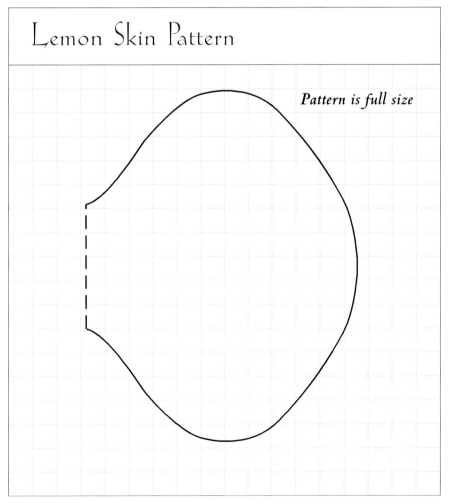

Lemon Skin Pattern

Pattern is full size

Tea Set

MATERIALS

+ *Plastic form or 2-inch (5cm) Styrofoam ball over which to form cup (I used a plastic container from a gumball machine that once held a small prize)*

+ *White tissue paper*

+ *White glue*

+ *Plastic wrap*

+ *Primer or gesso*

+ *Acrylic paint*

+ *Decorative paper scrap, (optional)*

+ *Lightweight cardboard (I used a paper plate)*

+ *Small balloon*

+ *Newspaper*

+ *Talcum powder*

+ *28-gauge craft wire*

+ *Small wooden bead*

+ *Gloss varnish or sealer*

Papier mâché lends itself to such a variety of uses. Here is a tiny tea service, which you can decorate with your own imagination.

CUP AND SAUCER

1. If using a Styrofoam ball to shape cup, wrap and tape a strip of paper around ball at midpoint to make cup sides. Dust form with a small amount of talcum powder. Cover form with plastic wrap, tucking excess inside form.

2. Tear white tissue paper into small pieces. In a small dish or container, dilute a small amount of white glue with approximately twice as much water to achieve a thin, brushable consistency. Lay the first piece of tissue paper on the form, and use a paintbrush to smooth it in place with the diluted glue. Continue layering tissue paper onto the form, smoothing each piece in place with the glue mixture until you have applied approximately three layers.

Set aside to dry. When piece is dry, apply three more coats of tissue paper and glue, setting aside to dry with each new coat.

3. Cut or tear a strip of tissue paper of approximately 1 by 10 inches (2.5 by 25cm). Lay craft wire on tissue paper and twist the paper tightly around the wire. Fold the twisted strip in half and again twist the two halves together. Shape the twisted piece into a handle approximately 1 inch (2.5cm) across. Wrap and glue a layer of tissue paper around handle and set aside to dry. Cut a 1-by-12-inch (2.5 by 30.5cm) and a 2-by-6-inch (5 by 15cm) strip of tissue paper. Form each strip into a tight twist. Trim top of dried cup to desired height. Glue thinner twist around the top of cup, even with edge, for lip. Glue the wider twist in a tight circle at bottom of cup for base. Trim handle, if necessary, and glue to side of cup. When handle joint has dried, apply a layer of tissue, and glue mixture over cup, smoothing over the joints of the lip, base, and handle. Let dry and repeat.

4. Transfer saucer patterns below to flat base of paper plate or cardboard and cut out. Butt short edges of rim and tape. Glue base to center opening of rim. Cut or tear a 1-by-14-inch (2.5 by 35.5cm) and a 2-by-6-inch (5 by 15cm) strip of tissue paper and twist each separately as before. Glue narrower twist just inside outer edge of rim for saucer lip. Glue wider twist in a tight circle around base of saucer for foot. When glue has dried, apply two or three coats of tissue paper and glue mixture to both sides of saucer. Set aside to dry.

5. Give saucer and cup each a thorough coat of primer or gesso and allow to dry. Paint as desired or follow my example in photograph on previous page, trimming with paper art and/or paint. When dry, seal with two or more coats of gloss varnish. Glue finished cup to center of saucer. Thread a ribbon or cord through handle for hanger.

Tea Cup Saucer Patterns

Patterns are full size

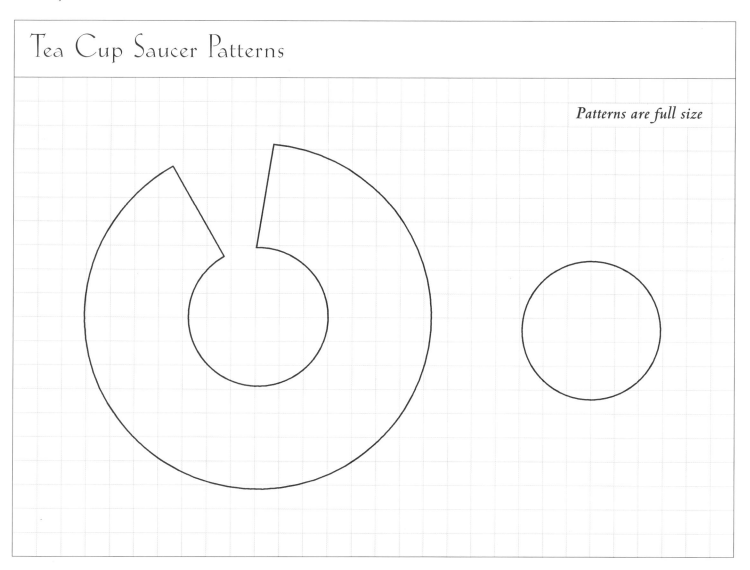

TEAPOT

1. Tear tissue paper into small pieces of approximately 1 inch (2.5cm). Inflate balloon to approximately 3 inches (7.5 cm) in height.

2. Dilute glue with water to a ratio of approximately 2 parts water to 1 part glue. Apply tissue pieces onto balloon with the glue solution used as sparingly as possible. You need to saturate the paper, but be aware that excess glue will take longer to dry. Working as quickly as possible, apply three layers of tissue paper and glue solution to entire balloon. Set aside to dry. When dry, apply another three layers of tissue paper and glue, allowing each new layer to dry.

3. Twist a strip of newspaper tightly to about the thickness of your pinkie finger. Cover the twist with plastic wrap. Cut a 3-by-10-inch (7.5 by 25cm) strip of tissue paper and wrap it around the plastic wrapped newspaper twist. Brush on glue solution to keep tissue paper in place and set aside to dry slightly. Meanwhile, cut or tear a 1-by-10-inch (2.5 by 25cm) and a 2-by-6-inch (5 by 25cm) strip of tissue. Twist each strip tightly. Wrap the shorter strip into a circle of approximately 1 3/8 inches (4cm) in diameter, trim ends of twist, and glue together. Glue to base of covered balloon. Wrap the longer strip into a circle of approximately 1 3/4 inches (4.5cm) in diameter, trim the ends, and glue together. Glue circle to top of covered balloon for rim of lid. Add two layers of tissue paper and glue over applied circles. Gently bend the drying tissue-covered newspaper twist to resemble a spout. Apply several layers of tissue, and glue to the spout, and set aside to dry.

4. Cut an 8-inch (20cm) length of craft wire and a 2-by-10-inch (5 by 25cm) piece of tissue paper. Twist the tissue paper around the wire, and then fold the covered wire in half, twisting the two halves together. Shape the wire into a teapot handle, and check it against the teapot. Trim if necessary. Cover with several layers of tissue paper and glue. You may want to rip a few narrower pieces of tissue paper for easier wrapping around the slim handle. Set the handle aside to dry.

5. When the spout has dried, slip it off the newspaper twist and, checking the teapot, trim the ends so that one fits the teapot and the other fits the spout. Glue the spout to the pot. When the glue has dried, apply several layers of tissue paper and glue to cover the joint. When the handle is dry, glue to the pot opposite the spout, add reinforcing tissue paper, and glue to hold it in place as with the spout. Set aside to dry.

6. Make a small hole at center top of teapot. Puncture balloon and pull out through hole. Layer and glue several pieces of tissue paper over the opening. When dry, glue a small wooden bead on top.

7. Apply a coat of primer or gesso to entire teapot. Paint as desired or follow photograph on this page. When paint is dry, add two coats of gloss varnish or other sealer. Thread ribbon through handle for hanger.

Mushroom

MATERIALS

- Lightweight air-drying clay (I used Crayola's Model Magic)
- Pencil
- Red, ivory, and green acrylic paints
- Spray sealer
- Small spring-type clothes-pin
- Glue

This perky clay mushroom mounted on a clothespin will create a bright spot of color against the dark green of a pine tree or wreath.

>-+‹›-O-‹›+-<

1. Shape a small piece of clay into a ball about 1 inch (2.5cm) in diameter. Roll ball between your hands until no seam lines show. Stick the eraser end of a pencil into the ball and use the pencil to roll the ball on your hand to shape the mushroom cap, slightly flatter and a bit conical. When you are happy with the shape, set aside to dry. When piece has set, take it off the pencil to dry completely. For the stem, use a piece of clay roughly half the size of that used for the top. Roll into a ball in the same manner as the cap, and then roll and flatten into a tube, making one end narrower, about the same width as the pencil. Set stem aside to dry.

2. When pieces are dry, paint the cap red and the stem ivory. Use a paintbrush end to paint dots on the cap. Refer to photograph. Glue the stem inside the cap.

3. Paint clothespin with dark green paint. When paint is dry, spray with two coats of sealer. When dry, glue mushroom to side of clothespin.

Sources

Aleene's Crafts in the Mail
P.O. Box 9500
Buelton, CA   93427

Good selection of glues, including foiling glues, foil, Duncan's line of paints, and other assorted crafting supplies.

D. Blumchen & Company
P.O. Box 1210
Ridgewood, NJ   07451-1210

Crinkle wire, wired tinsel garland, gold paper angel wings, metallic paper trims.

Cookie Art Exchange
P.O. Box 4267
Manchester, NH   03108

Stocks all Brown Bag Cookie Art molds and supplies for paper casting and beeswax molding.

Cherry Tree Toys
P.O. Box 369
Belmont, OH   43718-0369

Wooden shapes, animal cut-outs, pewter wheels, and assorted craft supplies.

Dover Publications, Inc.
31 East 2nd Street
Mineola, NY   11501

Publishes books of scrap art.

Holcraft
P.O. Box 792
Davis, CA   95616

A nice selection of chocolate molds both new and antique and helpful hints as to using them for wax, chalkware, papier mâché, etc.

Home-Sew
P.O. Box 4099
Bethlehem, PA   18018-0099

A good mail order source for metallic trims and a variety of sewing needs.

Keepsake Quilting
Route 25B, P.O. Box 1618
Centre Harbor, NH   03226-1618

An extensive selection of fabrics and some related crafting supplies, i.e., small clip-type clothespins.

Monterey, Inc.
P.O. Box 271
1725 E. Delavan Dr.
Janesville, WI   53546

A fantastic array of fake fur, (the sheep and squirrel tail fur came from here). They require a 1 yard minimum. Will send samples, contact them for current cost.

Newark Dressmaker Supply
6473 Ruch Road
P.O. Box 20730
Lehigh Valley, PA   18002-0730

Craft and sewing supplies.

New York Central Art Supply
62 Third Avenue
New York, NY   10003

Wide selection of specialty papers including metallic foils, also composition gold leaf and gold size.

Pearl Paint
308 Canal Street
New York, NY   10013

Good selection of craft supplies, paints including stained glass paints, glues, specialty papers, and papermaking supplies.

Index